Celebration Alchemy

Celebration Alchemy

A More Joyful Way to Live, Gather and Create Moments That Matter

Siobhán M. Hanley

Published by Game Changer Publishing

Artwork by Prasad Weerasinghe and Siobhán M. Hanley

Paperback ISBN: 978-1-969372-11-7

Hardcover ISBN: 978-1-969372-12-4

Digital ISBN: 978-1-969372-13-1

www.GameChangerPublishing.com

For my family and friends, whose love enriches my life.

And especially for Mom and Dad, Chun Ti and Brendie –

*Thank you for showing me that life's ordinary
moments hold so much magic.*

Your love of life and celebration lives on!

Thank You

Just to say thank you for choosing to spend time with my book.

As a token of appreciation, you'll find some bonuses
when you scan the code below.

Scan the QR Code Here:

Advance Praise
for the Author

"Siobhán finds light in the darkest rooms of life. Having navigated her own depths, she meets others in both grief and joy with profound empathy and strength. She is heart-centred, supportive and joyful."

— Marie Johnston, Peru

"Siobhán has a rare combination of joie de vivre, sensitivity and innate wisdom. She masterfully holds space for the moments that truly matter."

— Harinder Virdee, London

"Siobhán is made for this work – celebration is in her DNA."

— Julene and Richard, New Zealand

Celebration Alchemy

*A More Joyful Way
to Live, Gather and Create
Moments That Matter*

Life's Too Short Not To

Siobhán M. Hanley

Foreword

Since the beginning of time, we have had rituals for celebration. Everywhere in the world, regardless of class or culture, we come together to celebrate. This book provides you with an active guide to how you, as an individual, can contribute your energy to these celebrations. It also invites you to consider how we inhibit ourselves and the impact this can have.

Ultimately, it is a robust reminder of the importance of using celebration to live a more joyful, meaningful life.

It highlights how event professionals can bring this to life. You may start this book thinking, *I already know how to organise and design.* And you do. In the author's own words, *"This isn't about replacing what you know – it's about adding a new dimension to your practice. Something different, maybe intangible at times, but deeply powerful."*

When we work in events, we work in a deeply human industry. Yet, so often, we are focused on logistics and how to get things done, we lose sight of the *why*. At other times, we are so concerned about making the client "happy" that we lose sight of the expertise and soul we can bring to every event. If either of those feels familiar, this is the book to remind you that we are celebration alchemists and that our ideas, perspectives, and voices matter.

When we believe in the result that can be crafted, we can create something the client could not deliver without us.

When you have a true Irish soul exploring the magic of what we do, anchored deeply in being human and the suffering and challenges that will be part of life, you embark on a journey of soul. Life is complex, humans are complicated, and celebrations bring out all the complexities and toss them in front of us to be explored. It is in this space that we can bring out the best in our celebrations, for the people who are there to celebrate and be celebrated. Siobhán and her muse Celly show us the way.

There are many books that share how to deliver events, but none that invite you to undertake an examination of yourself and your motivations to live well and to celebrate with aplomb. "Wonder" and "joy" are not just words; they can – and we could argue must – be a way of approaching both life and celebrations. Even on the hard days.

A celebration is not designed on paper or video fly-throughs. It is designed in the hearts and minds of the designer(s). Celebrations must be meaningful, but that meaning comes from the mixology of designer and participant, individual and moment. It shouldn't feel easy, but it should have an ease when it comes to life. It should bring to the forefront moments that will be remembered forever, in stories told and retold, in images where the light shines through.

This is a book to be savoured. It invites you to examine your beliefs, open yourself to opportunities and push through the obstacles and attitudes that hold us back. It shares the adjustments that push us to heights we may only dream of. It reminds us that grief and joy intermingle, that listening is a skill to practise, and that one moment at a time, you can follow your inner guide and lead others to the places they want to be, celebrating with the people that matter most.

Follow Siobhán, and invite yourself, your teams, your clients and your friends to step into the magic of Celebration Alchemy that awaits!

—Tahira Endean

Author, *Our KPI is Joy: How Live Events Catalyze Happiness, Productivity and Trust* and *Intentional Event Design: Our professional opportunity*

Table of Contents

Foreword xi

Introduction I

SECTION 1 What Happened to Joy? II
Chapter 1 What Happened to Celebration?....................................13
Chapter 2 Message in a Bottle... 25

SECTION 2 From Flat to Fizz –
Reviving Joy, Celebration and Ourselves 49
Chapter 3 Joy, Shifts and Energy Flows (Oh My!) –
The Yellow Brick Road to Reconnection 5I
Chapter 4 Fizz by Design – The Life Mixology Method
to Reclaim Joy (and Celebration) 67

SECTION 3 Celebration 2.0 and The Spirit of Celebration 79
Chapter 5 Celebration Alchemy – The Art of Stirring Magic
and Spilling Joy 81
Chapter 6 Co-Celebration – Realising the Wonder of Us
and the Magic of We...99
Chapter 7 Living the Celebration Alchemist Way I27

SECTION 4 Celebration Alchemistry for Organisers –
Where Energy Meets Design 137
    Chapter 8 Celebration Alchemiser 139
    Chapter 9 Your Alchemising Oracle – SOUL Leadership
        in Action 155
    Chapter 10 SPARK Synergy 173

SECTION 5 Fizz, Flow and Full-Hearted Living 203
    Chapter 11 The Celebration (r)Evolution 205

EPILOGUE A Final Toast to My Dad 213

    Thank You! 215
    Celebration Alchemy A-Z Glossary 217

INTRODUCTION
Answering the Call of Celebration

There is a story behind this book, one I spent a lifetime searching for without realising it. For years, I chased personal transformation, meaning and connection. I studied, practised, and served. But I hadn't yet heard the one voice that would bring it all together: the voice of the Spirit of Celebration.

At first, she came in whispers: flashes of intuition, nudges towards joy, little winks from the universe. Then she grew louder: a clear, soul-deep tapping on my shoulder. She wasn't just an idea, a concept or a philosophy. She was (is) real. Sacred, yes. But as we got to know each other, I discovered she's also mischievous, playful and wildly alive. The kind of spirit who loves a boogie as much as a blessing. One who knows that true celebration is just as much about laughing until you cry – being spontaneous and feeling free – as it is about reverence, ritual and holding a loved one's hand through loss.

I came to know her as the "Spirit of Celebration." But somewhere along the way, especially in lighter moments, she became simply "Celly" – a sacred sidekick, a cheeky soul-friend, a joyful, untameable presence who can move me from tears to laughter, from seriousness to mischief. She reminds me that joy and sorrow, sacredness and play, are all part of the same beautiful dance of life.

Through her I understood I wasn't just called to study and share celebration – I was being invited to fully embody and live it for myself, to become Celly's emissary in the world. She even gave me a title: "Celebrationista." It's not in the dictionary (yet), but I knew what she meant because of my years in hospitality.

Like a skilled barista offering the perfect cup of coffee: evocative, hot, nourishing, artful, with perfect crema and made with love (can you tell I love coffee? I even wrote an ode to it once!). Or like a mixologist crafting the perfect cocktail: balanced, spirited, unexpected and just a little bit magical. The title and the role felt like a natural extension of everything I love and everything Celly was calling me to become. Over time, our relationship has deepened – something heartfelt, playful and alive. A practice, a pleasure, a devotion. I feel truly blessed.

But I didn't begin this book from a place of celebration. It came to me at a time when life felt impossibly hard. I was deep in grief: raw and hurting, feeling like life had worn me down. And yet, this book was a calling I could no longer ignore.

Now I know why. Through the very act of writing, I found myself connecting – truly, deeply – with Celly. She didn't just inspire these pages. She brought me on a journey that helped heal my heart.

Through her, I remembered that joy isn't just reserved for the easy, bright days. It's a decision, a practice, a willingness to find light even in the midst of sorrow. There were times she had me in tears, reliving precious memories. Times she held me in deep introspection, facing the places I had hidden from myself. And times she lifted me, laughing, and woke me back up to life.

She also reminded me that life is not about being perfect. It's about embracing ourselves – fully, wholly – as the beautiful, messy, glorious beings we are. And knowing that at our core, beneath all the forgetting, we are naturally wired for joy, connection and wonder.

This book is *celebration* reimagined: alive, intentional and transformational.

I call this repositioning "Celebration Alchemy™"– the art of transforming both everyday moments and milestone gatherings into something extraordinary. It's the energy and intention we bring that make the difference. This is how we reclaim the joy, magic and meaning we've lost. It's how we rise above burnout, performance and pressure. And it's how we remember who we are and bring that to life – moment by moment, gathering by gathering, heartbeat by heartbeat.

Celly, the Spirit of Celebration, my joyful, mischievous, gracious and generous guide

Celly and I invite you to walk with us on this journey.

Together, we'll explore what celebration truly means, why it matters now more than ever and how you can infuse it into your everyday life, on your terms, in your way. You'll move from the modern-day celebration crisis (Celebration 1.0) to a new paradigm grounded in alignment, intention and joy (Celebration 2.0).

Along the way, you'll experience powerful shifts: reconnecting with your own energy and truth, learning how to savour life, share joy generously and step into creative mastery. It's a path of Power, Pleasure, Possibilities and Purposeful Presence. Whether you're here for yourself or to guide others, this book is your invitation to remember, realign and reimagine what celebration – and life itself – can be *for* you and *through* you. This is both a bold shift and a natural unfolding.

I call it the (r)Evolution of Celebration.

What you'll find in these pages is the result of years of exploration, practice and refinement, a body of original work developed through lived experience and tested in real-world settings. Every model, tool and framework you'll meet here has been crafted and named by me to help bring this vision to life. I'm honoured to place them in your hands.

Let me introduce myself. I'm Siobhán Hanley. These days, thanks to Celly, I call myself the Celebrationista. It wasn't a role I applied for. It is a purpose I grew into, and, as I've come to realise, it's the expression of my true nature.

I come from a traditional Irish Catholic family, one of seven children, six brothers and me. (And no, in case you're wondering, I wasn't spoiled!) We ran a family business, and with a house full of brothers and rugby-mad cousins, life was lively, to say the least. My love for rugby ran so deep that I trained as a youth coach, became an accredited referee and an Irish Rugby Union official. It was part of why I felt drawn to move to New Zealand.

My career has been varied – spanning health services, government agencies, hospitality, tourism, rugby administration and events, with stints managing restaurants, ski lodges and festivals. My main gig has been leading corporate change management initiatives. If there is a common thread throughout, it is transformation: realising the potential of people, places and experiences.

But despite the variety and the achievements along the way, I continued to feel restless. As if there were a missing piece – a deeper purpose waiting just beyond the next project, the next role, the next success.

It wasn't until life turned me upside down, through personal losses too painful to name lightly, that I truly understood what was calling me. Grief cracked me open.

Losing my partner, my dad, my mum and my youngest brother in the space of a few short years brought me to my knees. Somewhere in the midst of the rubble, the Spirit of Celebration – my beloved Celly – began to whisper. Not with promises of easy fixes, but with invitations: to see joy even in sorrow, to honour what is, even when it hurts, to stop surviving and start living again.

It took time. For a long while, I did what many of us do: I kept going. I numbed out, overextended, masked the pain with a smile, buried it under productivity. But eventually, I found the truth: I wasn't broken; I was just disconnected: from myself, from joy, from life. That was the beginning of my real journey. I had studied positive psychology and well-being, building on my foundations in law, business, organisational change and human-centred design. Now, I went deep into the world of spiritual alchemy, super-conscious work and the beautiful art of being fully human.

The biggest lesson?

We don't need fixing. We just need to remember.

#MixNotFix became my new motto – a philosophy of wholeness rather than brokenness. Of curiosity and experimentation rather than resolve and control. Along the way, I've been blessed to learn from many brilliant teachers, including William Whitecloud, Michael Neill, Brené Brown and others, who helped me find my way home to myself. Their work, like bright stars in a dark sky, guided me back to a simple, powerful truth: We are already enough. Life is already worth celebrating. And we are wired for joy, if only we dare to remember.

#FizzByDesign is a reminder that we create our own joy. This book is part of that remembering. It's the story of how I reconnected with the Spirit of Celebration and how you can too. And in case you're wondering if it's too late to find your way back to joy. It's never too late. One of my personal inspirations, Louise Hay, didn't write her first book until she was sixty and went on to create a legacy that touched millions, and continues to do so. She believed that the rest of your life really can be the best of your life. Celly and I are here to remind you: it begins exactly where you are.

The Celebration Disconnection

When most people hear the word "celebration," they picture the big occasions: weddings, milestone birthdays, awards, anniversaries. The official stuff with balloons, cake, champagne and the like. But that's only part of the story.

Because celebration, at its heart, can be so much more.

I believe celebration, when adopted as a mindset and a practice, is one of the most liberating and powerful forces for good. One that's readily available as our birthright, as an innate part of who we truly are.

Yet we've been conditioned to forget that we are naturally wired for joy, playfulness, togetherness. You only have to watch a child lost in imagination, delighting in the simplest moments, to see it. That sparkle, that wholehearted way of living, was once second nature to us all. And then, slowly, it got buried. Not always intentionally or dramatically, but through busyness, expectations, disappointments, grown-up survival.

We disconnected from wonder and awe. We stopped noticing the magic in everyday life. We started waiting for "special enough" reasons to celebrate. And when those reasons finally came, we often found ourselves too stressed, distracted or self-conscious to truly savour them.

The Forgotten Legacy

Celebration is as old as humanity itself, woven into the fabric of culture and tradition for as long as we've gathered around fires and told stories under the stars. The word itself came later, but it continues that legacy, carrying the richness and importance that celebration has always held in human society. Its roots lie in the Latin *celebrare*: to honour publicly, to praise, to commemorate with both joy and sorrow. It's a rich tapestry of symbolism, ceremonies and rituals that mark thresholds and turning points, honour rites of passage, and acknowledge what truly matters to us.

Throughout history, people have always turned to communal celebration as a way to build belonging and trust, to pass down wisdom, express gratitude and strengthen community bonds. It's one of our oldest and most powerful tools for resilience, healing and hope. It has always been our way of staying connected – to each other, to life and to the greater spirit that weaves us all together. Never an optional extra, celebration in its purest form is a true expression of love – a lifeforce that enlivens us. Indeed, modern research confirms what our ancestors knew instinctively – celebration is good for us! It anchors meaning, strengthens relationships and boosts morale, well-being and resilience.

Why Celebration Matters (More Than Ever)

Yet we've lost touch with this wisdom, and it shows in how heavy life feels today. We're weighed down by stress, disconnection and relentless pressure. We've forgotten how to truly relax and enjoy life. Instead, we're increasingly isolated and fearful, caught in a downward spiral of disconnection – from joy and celebration – the very things we need now more than ever.

To reap the full benefit of celebration, we need to stop taking it for granted – simply going through the motions. When we choose to celebrate intentionally and wholeheartedly, we honour what we value most. At the heart of that is appreciation: recognising and savouring what's good in us and our lives.

And it's this shift in intention and perception that reconnects us to celebration as it's meant to be – our soul-fuel, our life force – revitalising us with renewed energy and purpose, making life feel richer, more connected, more alive.

Intention is powerful; that's why it's a fundamental element of Celebration Alchemy. When celebration is intentional, it becomes transformative: of gatherings, of people, even of sorrow and loss. Celebration Alchemy is about acknowledging and appreciating the meaning and magic of life. And this book is about bringing celebration – real, soulful, transformative – back to life. Not only for the big moments, but as a daily practice too. And not only for others, but for ourselves as well.

Appreciation, Gratitude and Celebration – What's the difference?

We often use the words appreciation, gratitude and celebration inter-changeably. But while they're connected, each plays a unique role in how we experience life. Think of them as distinct yet interconnected parts of a powerful cycle. Here's how I see them:

Appreciation is the foundation. It's the act of noticing, valuing and being present to what's already here. It's quiet, internal, moment to moment. Appreciation doesn't depend on receiving anything – it's a perspective you bring to the ordinary. It's the lens through which you spot and savour the good. Appreciation says, *"This matters."*

Gratitude is usually a response to receiving something: support, kindness, good fortune. It's more reactive, often tied to an exchange and focused on something external. Gratitude comes with the desire to give thanks to others or to life itself. But at times, it can slip into something we think we should feel, rather than something that arises naturally – and in those moments, it can lose its warmth. At its best, gratitude says, *"Thank you"* from the heart.

Celebration is the expression and ritualisation of both. It's how we acknowledge what we appreciate or feel grateful for. It can be loud or quiet, internal or shared, but it's always intentional. Celebration says, *"Let's fully feel and honour this."*

They're not always linear, but they do feed one another. Appreciation helps us notice what matters. Gratitude deepens our connection to it. Celebration lets us acknowledge and express it.

And when that cycle is alive, life feels richer. You notice more, feel more, savour more and want to share more with others.

The question, then, is this: if appreciation, gratitude and celebration are so powerful, why don't we experience them more often? Why do we feel awkward, disconnected or resistant to celebrating, when deep down, part of us longs to? That's something we're going to explore together.

The Journey Ahead

This book is about Celebration Alchemy: a new paradigm for living and gathering that puts joy, connection and meaning back at the centre of our lives. It's about moving beyond the old, surface-level approach to celebration into something richer, deeper and more life-affirming. It's about living as a Celebration Alchemist: someone who chooses to see and appreciate the extraordinary in the everyday.

You'll explore two core foundations that build on one another:

First, **Life Mixology** – understanding what makes us human so we can live more intentionally. It's about choosing to shift from default, reactive living into a way of being that's more conscious, connected and aligned with what you value.

Second, **Celebration Alchemy** – seeing and experiencing celebration not just as an event, but as a mindset and a practice. It blends appreciation, intention and energy to create moments that genuinely enrich life. You'll also discover the principle of **Co-Celebration** – the recognition that your energy always makes a difference. Whether you realise it or not, you're contributing your energy and influencing the overall vibe of every gathering you take part in. When you bring that awareness and choose to show up with intention, you help create experiences that feel more connected, generous and memorable for everyone.

And if you design or lead celebrations (events) – professionally or personally – you'll see how these two foundations come together in **Celebration Alchemistry**, where energy and intention meet design. You'll work with the proprietary **SPARK Synergy Framework** – a practical yet magical way to create celebrations that feel alive, connected and capable of delivering results beyond what logic alone might suggest. The kind that resonates deeply and leaves a lasting imprint, whether it's an intimate gathering or a large-scale event.

Each part builds on the last. So, whether you're here to enrich your own life, transform the way you celebrate with others, lead events in the new paradigm (or all of the above), you'll find the foundations, tools and inspiration to make it happen.

> Note: A wand ⁄ icon is used in the book to highlight practices and tools – simple ways for you to pause, reset and bring a little real-world magic into your celebrations and everyday life.

SECTION 1
What Happened to Joy?

Who Stole Our Fizz?

We're born knowing how to live joyfully with ease and instinct. No one needs to teach a child how to laugh, dance or marvel at the simplest moments. But as we grow up, that natural fizz begins to fade, slowly replaced by the pains and pressure of adulthood. Life starts to feel heavier. Expectations creep in, responsibilities pile on. What was once simple – expressing joy and celebrating – becomes complicated, tangled up in performance, perfection and permission. The effortless joy of childhood slips from our reach.

And it isn't just personal – it's bigger than that. As a society, we find ourselves living in fear, divided, quick to judge and reject what feels different or unknown. Prejudices, conscious or unconscious, keep us apart. Yet celebration has always held the opposite energy, power and purpose – to unite and connect joyfully. True celebration lowers defences, opens hearts and reminds us of our shared humanity. Where fear separates, celebration brings us back together.

This section looks at how this disconnection happened – and what it takes to rekindle the spark. To return to instinctive joy, genuine connection and the sacred spirit that lives inside every moment, if we dare to notice.

This is the call of the Spirit of Celebration. Let's answer it, together.

Chapter 1
What Happened to Celebration?

That Fizz Was Already Flat

The pressures of modern life haven't just dulled our joy, they've drained our energy. Beneath all the busyness and noise, something vital has slipped away – and one of the clearest mirrors of that loss is how we celebrate, or don't. When celebration feels flat or forced, it's not just a social problem; it reveals a deeper disconnection within and between us.

That's why I call it a modern celebration crisis. Not because celebration is the only thing damaged, but because it so clearly reveals that something deeper is out of sync. The way we gather reflects the way we live.

Why It's Not Just You: It's Modern Living

If you're feeling tired, disconnected or just over it these days, you're not alone. Modern life has become a pressure cooker of relentless strain, hustle, productivity and proving yourself. Our focus has shifted to simply getting through each day: juggling work, caregiving, grief, worry and endless responsibilities.

Everywhere we turn, the messages are the same:

> *Do more. Be more. Achieve more. Stay busy. Stay connected.*
> *Stay visible (especially online). Stay relevant – keep branding,*
> *keep posting, keep performing.*

But living like this comes at a cost, one we feel in our minds, our bodies and our hearts.

Modern Living: A Perfect Storm for Disconnection

Here's what we're up against:

- ❖ **Overdrive:** the glorification of hustle and exhaustion, at the expense of rest, presence and joy.

- ❖ **Hyper-Individualism:** the myth that we have to do it all alone, prove ourselves and look good doing it.

- ❖ **Distraction Overload:** a constant flood of noise, information and demands that fractures our focus and pulls us out of being present.

- ❖ **Techno-Stress:** the 24/7 barrage of notifications, comparisons and always-on expectations that exhausts and depletes us.

- ❖ **The Disconnection Epidemic:** digital contact without real connection, leaving more people than ever feeling isolated, lonely and unseen.

With all this going on, it's hardly surprising we feel like we're in survival mode. We do what we've been conditioned to do: keep going, power through, numb out, skip the pause, avoid the feeling.

How This Shows Up

When you're stretched thin and running on empty, the idea of celebration can feel like the last thing you have energy for. Even the thought of adding one more thing – even something meant to be joyful – can feel overwhelming.

And so celebration itself has become weighed down with guilt, pressure and misunderstanding. We've come to see it as a luxury: something optional, indulgent, even wasteful.

"I don't have the money." "I don't have the time."

We've come to see it as superficial, largely because of our social media-driven world of filtered perfection and constant comparison. Celebration has become more about appearances than authenticity, more of a performance for others than something meaningful for ourselves.

"It's all just showy. What's the point?"

And when it comes to celebrating ourselves, we often worry it will seem selfish or prideful, that it might make others uncomfortable, or open us up to judgement.

"I don't want to make others feel bad."

"They'll think I'm showing off."

We fear the fallout: that joy will be short-lived, leaving us exposed. Or worse, that it will come at a cost: the awkwardness, the comparison, the hangover, the crash.

In my work, I hear it again and again:

"I don't want to celebrate because of family drama."

"I dread birthdays. They just remind me of what I've lost (or how old I'm getting)."

"Weddings don't feel sacred anymore. They cost a fortune when the couple should be spending their money more wisely."

"I can't afford to go."

We don't associate celebration with joy. We link it with pressure, expectations, comparison and performance. Old wounds, limiting beliefs and hidden resentments get in the way.

The Result: Celebration Becomes Just One More Thing

And so, we ignore, avoid, or become blind to everyday magic altogether. We postpone celebrating, waiting for "someday" – for things to calm down, feel more certain, more deserved. But "someday" never comes.

Many of us have drifted into autopilot: either skipping celebration altogether or performing it in ways that don't truly nourish us. On the surface, it might look like we're in full party mode, but underneath, we feel empty.

When that happens, celebration loses its magic and potency. What was meant to feel joyful, meaningful and energising becomes flat and draining. The natural fizz of celebration – the spontaneity, warmth, connection – gets buried under layers of noise, expectation and exhaustion.

And it's not just the big occasions we miss, but the small ones too: the ordinary moments that could have been micro-celebrations, if only we'd noticed.

In losing our fizz, we lose a vital part of ourselves.

The Hidden Reason We Resist Joy and Celebration

We've seen the surface causes of disconnection, but there's also a more personal, unseen reason life feels this way – one that lives deep in our brain's wiring.

Throughout human history, staying alert to danger was essential to survival. Even now, we carry those ancient instincts into how we approach the good stuff: love, milestones, magic. It's why, even when something should feel joyful, we might find ourselves hesitating, guarding, bracing.

Before we explore new ways of celebrating, let's understand what we're working with. Our beautiful, protective brains sometimes get in the way of the very joy and ease we need most. But with a little awareness, we can begin to shift our everyday experience.

Your Brain's Protective Wiring

Our brain's survival system runs deep, rooted in the limbic system – the emotional centre designed to keep us alive. You might have heard it called the "reptilian brain." It's the oldest part of us, constantly scanning for threats and reacting quickly to danger.

In today's world, our brain still behaves as if predators lurk around every corner. It doesn't distinguish between *this tiger might eat me,* and *I'm anxious about being the centre of attention at my birthday party.* The imprint remains: scan for threats, even when life has moved on. That survival brain has a simple default: stay safe or be killed.

This is why, even when good things happen, our brains can struggle to trust them. Joy, visibility or vulnerability register as risks. The brain doesn't care if a perceived danger is social, emotional, or physical; it just wants to avoid pain. So instead of savouring the moment, we brace for hurt and disappointment.

This is called "**negativity bias**": our hardwiring gives more weight to negative events than to positive ones. The negative hits harder and lasts longer because negative experiences are like Velcro – they stick instantly and cling tightly. Positive experiences are like Teflon – they slide right off unless we consciously hold onto them.

This isn't because we're pessimistic or ungrateful. Our brains are built to detect danger, not dwell in delight. That's why a criticism haunts us, while a compliment barely registers. Why a mistake gnaws at us, but a success is quickly forgotten. Why we obsess over shortcomings, our own and everyone else's.

Why Celebration Can Feel So Risky (Even When We Crave It)

Celebration asks us to fully receive and trust the good – to pause, savour and express joy. But for many of us, that feels unfamiliar, even unsafe. Without realising it, we pull back, downplay our wins and rush past our milestones. We dampen our excitement, afraid it won't last, that we'll jinx it, or that others will judge us.

This constant vigilance crowds out gratitude and joy. The survival brain whispers, whether we're aware of it or not:

> *Don't relax yet. Something might go wrong.*
>
> *Don't get your hopes up. You'll only be disappointed.*
>
> *Don't celebrate too much. People will judge you.*
>
> *Look around. Everyone else is doing it better.*

Over time, this creates a quiet erosion. Moments that should lift us slip by unacknowledged. Achievements that deserve honouring get brushed aside. Connections that could deepen stay at surface level.

And when we add the collective climate we're living in – uncertainty, fear and instability – it's no wonder celebration feels even harder.

But if we really look, we might see something else: that celebration isn't a threat at all. It's a return to life – a remembering of what makes the hard parts worth it. It's exactly what we need: a remedy, not a risk. The antidote that helps us heal, reconnect and feel vital again.

Of course, knowing this doesn't make it easy to just say "yes" to celebration. Those deep protective patterns have been hardwired. So the real question is: can we do anything about it?

Yes, absolutely. But first, we need to understand what's really at play beneath the resistance.

Understanding What Triggers Us: The SCARF Model

Our internal radar is always on, quietly assessing what's around us: from interpreting a raised eyebrow to deciding whether it feels safe to enjoy a win or share joy. This radar influences how we feel, how we show up and how we experience the world.

That's why we sometimes feel tense, overwhelmed or oddly flat, even when nothing obvious seems wrong. Deep down, we yearn to live more fully – to feel connected and at ease – but our outdated survival programme keeps pulling us off balance.

To understand what's driving these responses, we turn to the **SCARF model.**

Developed by neuroscientist David Rock, SCARF outlines five key domains that drive human behaviour and influence our social experience. Each domain acts as a trigger, signalling the brain either towards safety into connection, or away from threat into self-protection. In simple terms: if something feels rewarding, we open up. If it feels threatening, we shift into defence mode.

Here's a quick snapshot of the five SCARF domains:

- ❖ **Status:** how important and valued we feel
- ❖ **Certainty:** how predictable and secure life feels
- ❖ **Autonomy:** how much control we feel we have
- ❖ **Relatedness:** how safe and connected we feel with others
- ❖ **Fairness:** how fairly and justly we believe we're being treated

Why It Feels So Personal (Because It Is)

We're wired to detect danger. But there's a subtlety: a perceived social threat triggers the same stress response as a physical one.

When you're excluded from a meeting, or someone doesn't respond to your invite, or you get feedback that hits a nerve, your body reacts as if your safety is at stake – a spike of stress, a gut punch of shame or hurt. These may seem like overreactions, but to your brain, social rejection registers as a threat to survival.

This is why those "invisible" social triggers can throw us so badly. They affect how safe, valued and connected we feel – and with that, how we show up, relate to others and experience life's most meaningful moments, including celebration. It also explains why, even when we long for joy and connection, we sometimes hesitate or hold back entirely.

By learning to recognise these unconscious reactions, we start catching the patterns that keep us stuck and can begin to choose differently. The good news is, the SCARF model helps us do just that – it lets us flip the script, actively creating more connection and joy (more on that later).

SCARF: Why Celebration Can Feel Risky

Let's look at how each domain gets triggered by celebration and what that reveals about our hidden resistance.

Status

Who Am I to Celebrate?

Status relates to our sense of worth or importance: how we see ourselves in relation to others. A perceived drop in status – being criticised, excluded or overlooked – activates the brain's threat response.

How this shows up in celebration

Celebrating can feel like drawing too much attention to ourselves. For many of us, this fear runs deep. Childhood messages like *"Don't get too big for your boots"* or *"Don't make a fuss"* still echo. Growing up in Catholic Ireland, I heard *"Children should be seen and not heard"* and *"Don't be making a show of yourself."* From a young age, we were conditioned to stay small, to keep under the radar, not to risk bringing shame on the family.

Standing tall feels risky, so it's no wonder we learn to downplay achievements, avoid praise, or shrink back from acknowledgement.

Certainty

What If It Doesn't Last?

Certainty reflects our brain's craving for predictability. To the brain, uncertainty signals danger.

How this triggers during celebration

Celebration makes us vulnerable. We think: *This feels too good to be true. What if this doesn't last?*

Psychologists call this "foreboding joy": the belief that if we allow ourselves to feel too good, something bad is just around the corner. So we pre-emptively protect ourselves from disappointment. But in doing so, we rob ourselves of joy.

Autonomy

I Don't Have a Choice

Autonomy is about agency: the freedom and choice we feel we have. Even small knocks to our sense of control can make us tense.

The celebration trigger

Sometimes celebration feels forced – weighed down with pressure, expectations, or indulgence that we never chose. *What if I don't feel like celebrating the way everyone else does? What if I can't afford it?*

When celebration feels imposed rather than freely chosen, resistance is only natural.

Relatedness

Do I Even Belong Here?

Relatedness is our need to belong: to feel safe and connected with others. When we sense rejection or exclusion, our nervous system flags major risk.

Why celebration can feel isolating

We usually think of celebration as social and positive. But for some, it stirs up fears of being left out or not fitting in. A tense family gathering, an awkward office party or a large event where it's easy to feel invisible can all bring up anxious questions: *Do I belong here? Will I have to pretend? Am I going to be a wallflower again?*

Rather than risk emotional discomfort, many opt out or hover just on the edges.

Fairness

I Don't Deserve This

Fairness taps into our deep need for justice and balance. When something feels unequal or unearned, it triggers guilt, shame or withdrawal.

How this dampens celebration

Many of us struggle to fully enjoy moments when we feel we haven't earned them, or when others around us are suffering. Thoughts like: *I didn't do enough. I can't enjoy this when others have it so hard.*

Cultural messages about humility and hustle only add to this. In a world where busyness is worn like a badge of honour, pausing to savour something can feel selfish or wrong.

Why This Matters

When any of these domains get triggered – even subtly – the brain reads celebration as a threat and kicks off the body's stress response. This explains why joyful moments (being celebrated, receiving praise, expressing gratitude) can sometimes feel oddly uncomfortable or even unsafe.

When we're operating from survival mode, we become hyper-vigilant, reactive, distracted and exhausted: the very opposite of what celebration is meant to evoke.

So if you've ever felt that inner pullback – hesitating, shrinking, brushing past the good moments – it's not a personal failing, it's an outdated survival script. But once you understand what's happening, you gain the power to shift it. You can catch those old stories as they arise and respond with choice, not just reflex.

The Modern-Day Celebration Crisis

I call this Celebration 1.0: how tarnished our current way of celebrating has become. It's the default mode many of us fall into without realising – celebration that adds to life's weight instead of lifting it.

When we fail to intentionally create space for life's precious moments, everything starts to feel heavier, more chaotic, more disconnected. Whether we realise it or not, we're collectively creating modern-day mayhem, one autopilot event after another.

Celebration 1.0: The modern-day celebration crisis –
a pressure cooker of stress, distraction and disharmony

We've seen how the brain's survival wiring triggers fear and insecurity, even in joyful moments. But that's only part of what's going on. To really understand why we do what we do, we need to look deeper – beyond the brain's scanning and old survival patterns and uncover what's actually driving them.

That deeper layer is your Inner Mix: the unique blend of beliefs, emotions, habits and patterns you carry inside you. We'll explore this in the next chapter through Life Mixology. But for now, it's enough to know that when you understand what's in your mix, you can start blending with intention instead of reacting on autopilot.

There's Another Way

This is exactly why I answered the call to reimagine celebration. With the Spirit of Celebration as my guide, I began to explore a different way – one that transforms not only how I approach celebrations, but how I live, connect and honour life itself.

Here's what I know: celebration isn't broken beyond repair. We're not broken either. We're distracted and disconnected – from ourselves, from each other, from what truly matters.

When we approach gatherings with intention, they become something far more powerful. Milestones become rites of passage. Events become portals. Moments become magical.

Whether it's a wedding, funeral, festival, retreat or milestone, there's a new paradigm waiting: one that honours life rather than adding to its pressure. One that invites real connection, meaning and, yes, a touch of magic!

That's the promise of Celebration 2.0 and Celebration Alchemy. But first, we need to understand what makes us human – not just our protective wiring, but our whole operating system.

That's where we're headed next.

Chapter 2
Message in a Bottle

What Are We Sending Out to the World (and Why)?

Inside each of us is a mix – our unique blend of beliefs, emotions, habits and patterns that colour every experience we have. I call it your *Inner Mix*. I find a bottle analogy helpful here. Like a bottle, the contents don't stay contained. They pour out into our relationships, our work, our lives.

This matters for celebration because your Inner Mix affects how you show up and engage at gatherings. Your unexamined mix can hijack even the most joyful moments.

Let's uncork your bottle and discover what's in your blend, so you can mix with more intention.

Why "Message in a Bottle"?

This chapter takes its title from the classic Police song. I chose it because it captures something we explored in Chapter One: how the modern celebration crisis leaves us feeling disconnected, unseen, isolated – like emotional castaways. The verse that lands hardest:

> *Walked out this morning, I don't believe what I saw.*
> *A hundred billion bottles washed up on the shore.*
> *Seems I'm not alone in being alone.*
> *Hundred billion castaways looking for a home.*

When celebration becomes pressure instead of pleasure, performance instead of presence, we end up broadcasting distress signals without realising it. We're constantly sending messages from the stories we carry about ourselves and what we expect from others.

Why? Because our brains, sensing threat, lock us into survival mode. When our core needs feel at risk (remember SCARF?), we activate protective scripts to keep ourselves safe. But these scripts cut us off from the very joy and connection we desperately need, keeping us stranded and silently sending out the same messages on repeat:

I'm fine. I don't need anything. I've got this. Leave me alone.

If we're not aware, it's easy to stay stuck in isolation. Maybe it's time to uncork your bottle and choose to send different SOS signals – ones of SOUL: openness, connection, gratitude and joy. Messages that reflect not survival, but a life lived in full colour.

To create new experiences, we first need to get curious about the patterns we've been repeating: where they come from, how they show up and how we show up with them.

What's in Our Bottle? Understanding Our Inner Operating System

There are countless books about what it means to be human in all its rich complexity. But for our purposes, we're keeping it simple, just the basics of what's driving your experience.

Let's start here: as humans, we're built to adapt. And we do that in two main ways – positively or negatively.

Positive Adaptation ensures we flourish. We evolve, transform and expand. Life feels spacious, possibilities open up, we're present, creative, connected. Celebration flows naturally from this state – it's our genuine "yes" to life.

Negative Adaptation leaves us stuck. We resist, defend and stagnate. Our world feels smaller, heavier, more constrained. We operate from survival mode, where celebration feels like pressure, performance or just another demand that weighs us down.

For so many, negative adaptation has become the new normal. And when that's your baseline, some important questions arise:

→ Why do some moments feel heavy while others flow?

→ What makes celebration feel draining instead of energising?

→ How does your inner state shape the energy you bring to gatherings?

→ What's in play when you walk into a room?

The answers lie in what's running your internal system – what's swirling inside your bottle.

We Run on a Hidden Programme

We operate on a hidden programme made up of thoughts, emotions, habits, beliefs and instincts. Most of the time, these run on autopilot – a script written from past experiences, survival instincts and absorbed conditioning.

Though invisible, it's powerful. That's why I want to walk you through this next part. When we understand what's really going on inside, we can take control of our journey and head towards more joy, meaning, connection and celebration.

Bottle Temperatures: SOUL and EGO States

A bottle's contents shift, fizz or settle depending on what's happening inside. In the same way, our inner life also has different "temperatures." At any given moment, we're operating from one of two core states – SOUL or EGO.

SOUL State

Sometimes, life feels like it's flowing. We're grounded, open, connected. Present, not racing. We respond with ease instead of reacting with fear. Our bottle temperature feels just right. The energy inside moves freely. We feel stable, spacious, alive. Celebration feels natural and nourishing. This is us living from our "Core Essence," positively adapting to life. I call this our

SOUL state, where we thrive and flourish. When we're here, we adopt the quality of FLOW mode *(see box)*.

S.O.U.L. State: Living from Core Essence

- ❖ Self-aware
- ❖ Open-hearted
- ❖ Unique
- ❖ Legacy-focused

F.L.O.W. Mode: Moving with Ease

- ❖ Flexible
- ❖ Light
- ❖ Optimistic
- ❖ Willing

EGO State

Other times, we feel tense, restless, on edge. Old survival patterns kick in. We become reactive and controlling. This is our EGO state; it's us negatively adapting: resisting and defending. Our bottle temperature swings to extremes. Sometimes it overheats, becoming overly fizzy, almost explosive – I call this RAVE mode. Other times it drops and we go numb, withdrawn, frozen – I call this FUNK mode. Neither extreme feels good for long, and neither state supports our health and well-being. Both are signs that we're stuck in survival mode: constricted and limited *(see box)*.

E.G.O. State: Stuck in Survival Mode

- ❖ Excessive
- ❖ Grasping
- ❖ Overthinking

R.A.V.E. Mode: Overheating *(Fight or Flight)*

- ❖ Reactive
- ❖ Agitated
- ❖ Validation-seeking
- ❖ Escaping

F.U.N.K. Mode: Freezing

- ❖ Fearful
- ❖ Unmotivated
- ❖ Numb
- ❖ Keeping small

Understanding EGO and SOUL

These two inner states determine how we experience and interpret life. Here's what's crucial: they're polar opposites, functioning like a switch. We can't operate from both at once. We're either triggered and reactive (EGO) or open and in flow (SOUL).

This matters because whichever state we're in colours everything: how we see ourselves, how we relate to others, what we notice, what we miss. Even what possibilities we can imagine or allow.

It's important not to label EGO as "bad" – it's just doing its job to protect us. It's constantly scanning for danger, doing its best to keep us safe. The problem is that protection is false. It keeps us small, limited and ultimately costs us what we truly long for: joy, connection and celebration.

The Shadow

There's something else bubbling away inside the bottle too, silent but powerful. It's the parts of ourselves we've pushed down, hidden or forgotten over time: the bits that once felt too much, too messy or unwelcome. Sometimes these show up as old wounds; other times as strengths and gifts we didn't realise we'd packed away.

This is the "Shadow." Unlike SOUL or EGO, it isn't a state we switch into. It's more like an invisible ingredient, subtly flavouring the whole mix. Even if we're not aware of it, our Shadow colours how we show up – what we highlight, what we avoid, what we keep hidden.

Later, we'll explore how meeting your Shadow and learning to work with it alongside EGO and SOUL can transform the entire flavour of life and celebration. For now, it's enough to recognise that something unspoken may be influencing your experience. That noticing alone can shift how you see yourself and how you show up to celebrate.

The Next Layer: Awareness

Now that we've explored the "temperatures" of our bottle – whether we're flowing, fizzing or freezing – there's another layer to consider. Before we look more closely at all the different ingredients inside, we need to ask a crucial question:

How much of it are we actually aware of?

Because whatever's swirling inside, awareness is everything. It's not just about what's there, but how conscious we are of it. That awareness is what decides whether we stay on autopilot or make real choices about how we live and celebrate.

How "Awake" Is Your Bottle?

If your body and mind are the container – your bottle – then the charge inside is your consciousness: your aliveness in motion. The strength of that charge reveals how awake and aware you are in any moment.

Consciousness isn't just one thing; it's layered, with different depths influencing what we experience.

Sometimes your consciousness sits dormant at the bottom, everything still and sealed – like when we're just going through the motions, not questioning why we do what we do.

Sometimes, it stirs in the middle, gently active – like when you sense something needs attention but can't quite name it yet.

Other times, it's fully active at the surface – those moments when an insight hits and you suddenly see something in a completely new way.

And occasionally, it surges beyond the bottle entirely – those breakthrough moments of deep knowing, connection, or creativity when you feel fully in flow with life.

Consciousness and awareness are closely linked, but they aren't exactly the same. Consciousness is the broader state – the charge, the aliveness running through everything. Awareness is the specific moments of clarity that punctuate it – the "noticing" that something has shifted or surfaced.

What we've been describing – from dormant states to full breakthroughs – line up with what psychologists describe as the **four levels of consciousness:**

- ❖ **Unconscious**
- ❖ **Subconscious**
- ❖ **Conscious**
- ❖ **Superconscious**

This matters because without consciousness, without being truly present to what's going on inside, it's almost impossible to course correct. And we miss out too: moments of clarity, inspiration and creativity can slip past if we're not awake to them.

The problem is, when we're stuck in survival mode, consciousness tends to contract, and awareness is usually the first thing to go. And without awareness, we can't change anything.

Let's take a closer look at these four levels.

Understanding Consciousness: A Practical Map

Consciousness can be mapped in many ways – neuroscience, psychology, spirituality. The four-level model I use here is practical, grounded in both research and my coaching work. Intuitive coaching frameworks recognise the superconscious level as a source of insight and guidance, which aligns with what I call living from SOUL.

Think of these four levels as different ways the charge inside your bottle behaves.

I. The Unconscious Mind: Our Inner Autopilot

What it is: The foundation of our experience, operating beneath awareness. It has two aspects: the physiological (heartbeat, breathing, reflexes that keep us alive) and the psychological (instincts, survival responses, ingrained beliefs and habits). It's this psychological unconscious – our conditioning, our patterns – that shapes our behaviour in powerful, persistent ways, often before thought or choice. Most of these patterns are protective and automatic, which means they tend to run in EGO mode.

Why it matters: While the physiological unconscious keeps us alive and functioning without effort, the psychological unconscious drives behaviours, fears or reactions that feel like they come out of nowhere. These learned patterns affect how we show up and celebrate, often without us realising. That's why we sometimes act in ways that even surprise us.

Bottle analogy: At this level, the bottle is sealed tight. We don't notice the temperature shifts or pressure building inside from old patterns and conditioning until it bursts out as our reactions: snapping at someone, shutting down, or feeling flat, even in moments meant to be joyful.

2. The Subconscious Mind: The Pattern Keeper

What it is: The subconscious stores information and processes our learned patterns: everything we've internalised about who we are, how the world works and what's possible. It's like a mental filing system running in the background. It doesn't question or analyse; it simply runs what's been programmed or filed. Left unchecked, it reinforces EGO loops and limiting scripts.

Why it matters: Think of it as your mental assistant, helping you function efficiently by handling routine tasks and making connections you don't consciously think about. It can bring forward useful information or forgotten memories when triggered. This makes life easier – you don't have to relearn everyday tasks – but it also means unhelpful scripts repeat unless you pay attention. The good news is that, unlike the unconscious, these patterns can be accessed and adjusted when you bring awareness to them.

Bottle analogy: The bottle has a screwcap now, sealed but adjustable. The pressure and temperature inside still build, and if left unchecked, the results look just like the unconscious level, bursting out in familiar reactions. But here there's a crucial difference: the screwcap means you can access the flow and begin to adjust it, opening up the possibility of different outcomes.

3. The Conscious Mind: The Decision Maker

What it is: This is your current awareness, what you're actively thinking about, feeling and experiencing right now. It's where you make deliberate decisions, solve problems and engage with the present moment.

Why it matters: This is your control centre for intentional action and reflection. It's your "spotlight of attention," focusing on whatever you choose – a task, a thought, a feeling. It's where you learn, adapt and bring new understanding into how you live. It's where you can pause, question what's driving you and consciously choose your response. In other words, it interrupts autopilot and guides how you engage with life.

Bottle analogy: At this level, the bottle is open. You can sense what's inside as it begins to pour. There's still pressure from deeper patterns, but now you can regulate the flow: pausing, redirecting or choosing what to release. This is the space where awareness gives you agency over what, and how much, you pour.

4. The Superconscious Mind: Our Higher Self

What it is: This is the realm of insight, intuition, creativity and a deep sense of connection to something greater than ourselves. It's what we might call our soul, higher self or inner knowing. At this level, we're no longer driven by fear or conditioning, but guided by clarity, purpose and presence. Life feels expansive, aligned and rich with meaning.

Why it matters: The superconscious is where inspiration and wisdom come alive. It's the space of flow states, peak experiences, breakthroughs and moments of deep connection that feel bigger than us. It's where we access the energy to create in ways that feel magical, meaningful and transformative.

Bottle analogy: This is when the charge flows, naturally and freely, with loving expansion. The energy moves beyond the bottle, purposely spilling joy and appreciation into the world.

Why the Subconscious Matters Most for Celebration 2.0

All four levels of consciousness influence us, but the subconscious plays a particularly powerful role in shifting how we relate to life and to celebration.

As we've seen, the subconscious doesn't reason or judge. It simply accepts and reinforces whatever you repeatedly feed it. This is why the beliefs and stories you've internalised about celebration influence your experience so profoundly.

If you've absorbed messages like:

> *I don't deserve to celebrate.*

> *Celebration is selfish, indulgent, unnecessary.*

> *There's nothing worth celebrating right now.*

> *I don't have the time, money or energy to celebrate.*

Then your subconscious filters reality through those clouded lenses. And because it looks for proof of what it already "knows," it will magnify your experiences that confirm the belief – ramping up stress, glossing over joy – just to validate: *There's nothing worth celebrating,* or more damaging, *I'm not worth celebrating.*

The Encouraging Part

Your subconscious doesn't distinguish between real and imagined experiences. Every image, word and emotion you repeat becomes a signal about what's true for you. When you consciously choose to focus on what's life-affirming – appreciation, connection, moments of ease or beauty – you start teaching your inner world a new story.

The more vividly you imagine and feel those experiences, the more your mind and body register them as real. In this way, noticing, appreciating and celebrating – even the smallest things – begins to rewire your brain and reprogramme your subconscious. Each micro-moment of genuine emotion strengthens the pattern.

This is why celebration isn't indulgent. It's transformative. It's literally retraining your nervous system to recognise and hold joy.

Your Inner Mix: What's Really Inside the Bottle

So far, we've explored the two operating states (SOUL and EGO), the Shadow, and the deeper forces that influence how we experience life: our levels of consciousness. Now, it's time to take an even closer look inside the bottle. Because beyond the state we're operating from and beyond our level of awareness, there's something else at play: your "Inner Mix" – the unique blend of components that influence how you feel, how you relate, how you behave and, yes, how you celebrate.

Elements like our mindset, beliefs, emotions, thoughts, habits and personality aren't just passive traits. Each one has the power to either anchor you in SOUL and help you thrive, or pull you deeper into EGO's patterns of fear, control, overwhelm or shutdown. These components don't operate in isolation. They swirl together, reinforcing your state, forming your stories and colouring your experience of life.

And the more clearly you can see what's happening inside – what's driving you, what's supporting you and where you might need a remix – the more choice you have about how you arrive, how you celebrate and how you live.

Human Components Framework

Here's a framework to help you understand the key components that make up your Inner Mix. How each part operates depends on your state – whether you're aligned in flow or stuck in resistance. By exploring each one, you'll start to notice your default settings, your hidden habits and the leverage points that offer the most room for transformation.

Even small shifts can flow outward and change everything – your energy, your impact, your experience. So it's worth spending some time here. Each component is explored in more detail after the table.

This isn't about judgement; it's about awareness and intention. So, please be patient and kind with yourself. In this way, each of your components can become a doorway to alignment.

Components of Our Inner Mix

Experience Component	SOUL (Aligned Self)	EGO (Survival Self)	Shadow (Suppressed Self)
Personality	Protective mask falls away, essence shines, presence is enough	Managed self-image, seeking approval and validation	Repressed traits can resurface as sabotage or hidden gifts
Mindset	Growth-oriented, possibility-focused	Fixed, fear-driven, defensive	Inner doubts can restrict or reveal possibilities
Beliefs and Perception	Expansive, flexible, empowering	Constricted, rigid, resistant, limiting	Hidden stories and lens can distort or seed resilience
Thinking Self	Clear, intuitive, insightful	Over-analytical, controlling, anxious	Thoughts can trap or reveal intuition
Emotions	Embraced and used as guidance for clarity	Suppressed or exaggerated to maintain control	Buried feelings can overwhelm or be a path to deeper empathy

Experience Component	SOUL (Aligned Self)	EGO (Survival Self)	Shadow (Suppressed Self)
Feelings	Peaceful, appreciative, connected	Stressful, avoidant, fused with old resentments	Old hurts can stay painful or fuel awareness
Mood	Calm, grounded, uplifting presence	Heavy, tense, reactive energy	Moods can trigger or transform
Behaviours and Habits	Intentional, values-aligned, purposeful	Automatic, reactive, pattern-driven	Motivation can sabotage or support

The Components

Personality

Personality is the distinctive pattern of thinking, feeling and behaving that characterises how we show up in the world. It gives us our unique flavour: the traits and tendencies that others recognise as "you."

Although personality isn't fixed, it does stay relatively consistent because it's been formed from patterns of behaviour and beliefs that helped us feel safe, accepted or in control. Over time, these patterns can harden into a kind of armour – useful for protection, but limiting when mistaken for the whole of who we are.

With self-awareness, we begin to see that personality is learned identity that's adaptable. It's a helpful navigation tool, but not our whole self. The real work isn't about labels or boxes; it's about loosening the grip of old defences and reconnecting to SOUL – the essence beneath the persona.

One model that supports this exploration is the Enneagram: a map of nine personality patterns, each formed by different ways of seeking love, safety or belonging. Used with compassion and curiosity, it helps us notice when we're on autopilot and guides us back to what's most authentic and alive within us.

Why it matters: Personality colours how you see yourself and how others experience you. If you're not aware of your patterns, they're running the show. Awareness brings choice, and with choice comes freedom – the freedom to soften old compensating strategies, make conscious decisions and lead from essence rather than defence.

In celebration: Personality sets the initial tone when you walk into a room. But it's only one part of the energy you bring. The deeper impact comes when your presence reflects who you truly are, not a role you've adopted. Celebration becomes most powerful when it flows from integration – when personality, essence and intention are all in sync. That's the heart of Celebration Alchemy. For now, simply noticing how your personality patterns influence the space around you is a powerful first step. It helps you choose how you want to arrive and opens the door to more authentic, connected, joyful moments.

Mindset

Your mindset is how you make sense of the world. It's the filter that colours how you engage with life, how you interpret experiences, respond to challenges and imagine what's possible.

Psychologist Carol Dweck describes two main types of mindset: "fixed" and "growth." Simply put, a fixed mindset sees traits and talents as set in stone: You're either good at something, or you're not. A growth mindset, on the other hand, sees potential as expandable: You can learn, adapt and grow through effort and feedback. That distinction and understanding become especially vital when you're stretching yourself. Your motivation and attitude are tested most as you take on new challenges.

Why it matters: Mindset is the base note in your Inner Mix; it flavours everything else. If it's fixed and fear-based, you'll see everything as a challenge and every challenge as a threat. You'll play it safe or opt out altogether. But when your mindset is rooted in growth, you see those same challenges as invitations. You're curious and open to experimenting, adjusting and evolving.

In celebration: Mindset determines whether you approach celebration as something to avoid or endure or as something to enjoy. A fixed mindset might cling to how things "should" look, how people "should" be, or be afraid of getting it wrong. But a growth mindset invites play, curiosity and a willingness to let the moment unfold, even if it's imperfect. It turns pressure into possibility and allows celebration to be pleasurable, enjoyable and life-enhancing.

Beliefs and Perception

Beliefs are deep-seated stories about who you are, what's possible and how the world works. Most form in childhood, often in moments when your needs for love, safety or belonging felt unmet. From there, you spend much of your life trying to resolve, fix or compensate for that early sense of lack.

These beliefs usually run beneath your awareness, quietly steering how you see yourself and what feels possible. Naming them can be a powerful reference point on the self-awareness journey, but don't waste energy trying to fix them. The real work is to notice when they're at play. That moment of awareness begins to loosen their grip and restore choice.

Perception, on the other hand, is how you interpret what's happening right now. It's filtered through your beliefs, emotional state and past experiences. It isn't fact, but it feels true. When you're under pressure or stress, perception tends to narrow, focusing more on threat than possibility.

Two people can experience the exact same moment and walk away with completely different interpretations. That's the power – and the pitfall – of perception: it doesn't create the truth, only your version of it. Depending on your Inner Mix, that version can be helpful, generous and authentic ... or defensive and distorted.

Why they matter: Limiting beliefs – *I'm not enough, I have to earn love* – silently restrict your choices, keeping you on edge, waiting or striving. When you become aware of these hidden filters and lenses, you can start to question the old assumptions and catch the limiting stories that narrow your view. You see the lens of perception for what it is, instead of unquestioningly looking through it. That awareness is what loosens the hold and brings you back to choice.

In celebration: Beliefs and perception influence how you approach celebration – whether you welcome it, resist it or overdo it. If you've absorbed the story that celebration is self-indulgent, even a simple party invite might trigger guilt or discomfort. If your belief says, *I don't deserve to be acknowledged,* being celebrated may feel deeply uncomfortable, even when it's meant with love.

Once you catch a belief, or see the lens, you can begin to tell yourself a new story: *This matters. I'm allowed to enjoy it. I don't have to earn it.* That's not blind positivity – it's freedom. The power to respond from choice rather than conditioning.

Thinking Self

Your "thinking self" is the running commentary in your head, the mental narrator. It's the voice that compares, plans, doubts, imagines and sometimes catastrophises. It includes your conscious thoughts and inner dialogue, and also the deeper loops and stories humming just below awareness. These thoughts aren't always rational or kind, but they are powerful. And unless we pause to check in, we tend to believe all of them.

Why it matters: Thoughts determine how we interpret reality. The same event can feel completely different depending on the story we're telling ourselves about it. Clear, grounded thinking creates space, presence and possibility. Tangled thinking, caught in fear or assumptions, sends us spiralling. Unchecked, it keeps us in survival mode. But conscious awareness of thought opens the door to SOUL FLOW. Sometimes, the greatest gift you can give yourself is a pause, a moment of quiet where clarity and insight can rise.

In celebration: Celebration invites presence, connection and spaciousness, a moment to feel the joy of being alive. But that's hard if your mind is on overdrive: rehearsing conversations, bracing for awkwardness or worrying whether you're doing it "right." That isn't celebrating, it's just struggle and survival.

Your thoughts can either anchor you in what's meaningful – helping you savour, appreciate and show up authentically – or pull you into performance mode, focused on how you think others might be perceiving you. They can magnify joy or muffle it completely. When you pause, breathe and check in with your thoughts, you create space to reconnect with what the moment is really about. That's where the magic of celebration lives.

Emotions

Emotions are the body's fast, instinctive responses to what's happening in the moment. They arrive before your thinking mind has caught up – flashes of heat, tension, excitement or unease. You don't choose them; they simply show up, like messengers at the door.

Why they matter: Emotions are your first responders. If you're not paying attention, they can take over. But when you notice and name what you're feeling – without suppressing it or letting it explode – you tap into emotional intelligence. The ability to recognise what you're feeling, manage your response and stay present with what others are experiencing.

In celebration: During celebrations, emotions can run high – before, during and after the event. Pressure, expectations, vulnerability, joy and even grief can swirl together. If you're not mindful, a single moment – a comment, a forgotten detail – can hijack the whole experience.

Emotions are contagious. Your anxiety spreads. So does your calm. When you notice what you're feeling and choose how to respond, you change not just your own experience but the atmosphere for everyone. That awareness is what keeps a tense moment from becoming a meltdown, or lets a small gesture become magical.

Feelings

Feelings are the longer-lasting, meaning-laden companions of emotion – the undercurrent that lingers after the initial wave has passed. Unlike quick, instinctive emotions, feelings form from our thinking, our interpretation of an event. They're influenced by memory, beliefs and our inner narrative. Feelings are personal, conscious and rich with meaning.

Why they matter: Unprocessed feelings don't disappear. They settle in your body as tension, fatigue or restlessness. They leak out as irritability, withdrawal or people-pleasing. When you can't name what you're feeling, it runs the show from the shadows.

But here's what changes everything: *language.* Researcher Brené Brown calls this "naming to tame" – the simple act of putting words to what you're feeling reduces its grip. You don't have to fix the feeling or make it go away. Just naming it – *I'm anxious, I'm overwhelmed, I feel unseen* – shifts something. It moves the feeling from a vague, consuming fog into something you can actually work with.

In celebration: Feelings colour how you show up. Anticipation, pressure, gratitude or dread – whatever lingers beneath the surface influences your presence and how you celebrate. When you pause to name what you're feeling, you create space to choose your response. That recognition may not change the situation, but it can absolutely change how you experience it.

Mood

Mood is the emotional climate you carry, not a single sharp feeling, but the overall atmosphere of your presence. While emotions are quick flashes and feelings are layered with meaning, mood is the low hum in the background, the energetic weather system you bring into a room. Moods are influenced by everything: your recent feelings, past experiences, stress levels, physical well-being, even the weather. They tend to stick around, casting a filter over how you perceive and respond to everything.

Why it matters: Mood is contagious. Walk into a room anxious and edgy, and others pick it up before you've said a word. Arrive calm and grounded, and that steadiness spreads too. You're not responsible for managing everyone's experience, but you are influencing it – whether you realise it or not.

In celebration: Your mood has the power to lift a space or cast a shadow over it. You don't need to fake being "fine," but noticing your mood gives you the chance to reset. A few deep breaths, a moment outside, a shift in focus – small recalibrations can transform the atmosphere you're creating. You get to choose what you bring, and that choice spreads outward.

Behaviours and Habits

Behaviours are your visible actions and reactions – what others see and experience. Habits are the patterns behind them: routines repeated so often they've become automatic.

Some habits are practical (how you start your day). Some are emotional (how you react under pressure). Others are mental (how you talk to yourself). Many began as coping mechanisms – ways to feel safe, in control or accepted. Some still serve you, others may quietly hold you back.

Here's how they connect: a habit of needing certainty might show up as over-planning every detail. A habit of self-criticism might look like apologising excessively. The habitual pattern runs beneath; the behaviour is what others experience.

Why they matter: This is where your inner world becomes visible. When you spot patterns that no longer serve you, you can begin to remix them – one small shift at a time. And you can deliberately build new ones: pair an existing habit (brushing your teeth at night) with a new practice (naming one good thing from your day). Tie them together and the new practice sticks. This isn't about being perfect or forcing change; it's about making it easier to choose what supports you.

In celebration: How you move through a celebration – rushing or present, controlling or easeful – sets the tone for everyone. Old patterns like micro-managing, people-pleasing or pre-emptive apologising turn celebration into something to survive rather than savour.

When you notice the pattern, you can choose a different action. Pause instead of push. Breathe instead of brace. Ask for help instead of carrying everything alone. Small, intentional shifts change not just how the moment feels, but what it means – and whether you're creating connection or chaos.

Using the Framework

The Human Components Framework helps you see what's happening beneath the surface, spot patterns and reconnect with your wholeness. You don't need to analyse every part of yourself. What matters is noticing when something feels off, pausing to check in and see what's at play.

If you suddenly feel tense, irritated or shut down, it's often a sign something deeper is stirring – a belief, a thought loop or an old pattern being triggered. You don't need to fix it or figure it all out on the spot. Just catching yourself in the moment can create enough space to choose differently. A pause and a deep breath can shift how you respond. That's what I call "mixing with intention."

Often, the deeper understanding comes later, when the moment has passed and you explore what was underneath. Journalling is one of the most powerful ways I know to peel those layers with compassion and curiosity.

You start to see patterns not as problems to fix but as things to understand. You recognise the story behind them and realise they no longer need to run the show. You begin to see it solely as "information." That awareness lets you release the charge (and its hold over you) and reconnect with SOUL expression, embracing possibilities. That's when freedom begins – you respond from wholeness, more and more naturally.

So how do you actually use this framework? How do you start working with the Inner Mix in a real and practical way?

While every component plays a role in how we experience life, not all of them carry equal weight. Some act as leverage points. In my experience, there are three big-hitter areas – the components where even a small adjustment changes the whole flavour:

Mindset: *The Filter That Colours Everything*

Beliefs: *The Scripts Running in the Background*

Emotional Flow: *The blend of Emotions, Feelings and Moods*

Think of these as your power ingredients *(see box)*.

The Three Big Hitters: Your Quick Action Guide

Mindset – The Filter That Colours Everything

> → What to watch for: Fault-finding, self-judgement, "proving" energy.
>
> → Quick shift: *Ask What would a growth mindset say here?*
>
> → Try this: Replace *I have to get this right* with *I'm learning as I go.*

Beliefs – The Scripts Running in the Background

> → What to watch for: That pressure to say yes, perform or keep the peace.
>
> → Quick shift: Notice and name it – *Ah, there's that old script again.*
>
> → Try this: *This belief once kept me safe, but it no longer serves me.*

Emotional Flow – Emotions, Feelings and Moods

> → What to watch for: Reactive moments, energy shifts, "off" feelings.
>
> → Quick shift: Pause and ask, *What's showing up right now?*
>
> → Try this: Use the SNAP Check-In (over) to reset and choose how you want to show up.

 The Power Move – These three work together. When you feel stuck, reactive or "off," ask:

> → *What filter am I using right now?* (Mindset)
>
> → *What old script might be playing?* (Beliefs)
>
> → *What energy am I carrying?* (Emotional Flow)

Remember: you're not trying to fix anything; you're choosing how to respond.

Emotional Flow

We just named Emotional Flow – the blend of emotions, feelings and moods – as one of the three big hitters in your Inner Mix. These three terms are often used interchangeably, but they're not the same. Knowing how they differ and how they work together gives you real power over your energy and presence.

Here's how they differ, and why they work together:

> → **Emotions** are *outside-in:* quick body reactions (e.g., a flash of heat, tension, excitement).

> → **Feelings** are *inside:* the meaning you give those emotions (e.g., dismissed, overlooked, appreciated).

> → **Moods** are *inside-out:* the vibe that lingers and colours the room (e.g., low-key resentment others can pick up).

Put simply, emotions reflect how the outside world impacts you, while moods are the effect your inner world has on those around you. And because they build on each other, one small pause can interrupt the flow before it runs the show. That's where the SNAP Check-In comes in.

SNAP is what happens when we don't pause – and it's also the pause itself. Here, "snap" becomes your moment of awareness, agency and choice.

⟋ **SNAP Check-In™: When You Feel Off-Centre**

A four-step reset for when you need to interrupt autopilot and reclaim choice:

Sense in; Name the story; Ask a better question; Pivot.

Use SNAP any time you feel reactive, heavy or out of alignment, before an important meeting, walking into a celebration or during a tough day.

> ❖ **S: Sense in – How am I showing up right now?**
> Pause and notice what's present emotionally, mentally, physically. No judgement, no fixing, just sensing:
>
> *I feel tense and a bit shut down.*
> *There's a heaviness I hadn't noticed until now.*
> *I feel buzzy and restless, like I'm not quite here.*

❖ **N: Name the story – What am I telling myself?**
Notice the narrative running under the surface. What belief or perception might be influencing how you feel? Naming it loosens its grip:

I'm telling myself I don't belong here.
Nothing fits right, and I already feel ashamed.
I feel like I have to fake being upbeat or I'll ruin it for others.

❖ **A: Ask a better question – Is that the whole truth?**

Challenge the story instead of accepting it at face value. Curiosity shifts perspective. Even one new question can open space for possibility:

Is this simply discomfort, not danger?
Is this dread, or is there excitement underneath?
What would it be like to show up just as I am?

❖ **P: Pivot – What would support me right now?**
Choose something different. A small shift that feels more aligned:

This time, I'll choose something comfortable and focus on enjoying myself.
Maybe I'll arrive early and see if I can help.
I'll pause, breathe, and let myself be real.

SNAP works best with a few deep breaths and plenty of self-compassion. Even if you forget the steps, simply pausing and noticing is already powerful.

From Awareness to Intention

We've just taken a close look inside your bottle. You've uncorked what creates your vibe: your operating states (SOUL, EGO and a whisper of Shadow), your levels of consciousness and the many components of your Inner Mix: personality, patterns, emotions and more.

You've glimpsed what's been bubbling beneath the surface, and the way that mix flavours how others experience you – in life and in celebration. No judgement needed or invited. This is about self-awareness, and all we're aiming for right now is insight. Because insight is the first ingredient in transformation.

I mentioned that I use cocktail and mixology metaphors as my framework for transformation, and we're nearly there. But before we go full mixologist mode, there's something important to understand: you've been mixing all along. Whether you realise it or not, every thought, every feeling, every behaviour – everything we've covered in this chapter – has been part of your life's recipe so far. This is your first taste of Life Mixology 101. And yes, sometimes, what we've been shaking up (mostly unconsciously) might be a little off – a survival-style blend of stress, pressure, people-pleasing or avoidance.

We'll explore this in more detail shortly. For now, just know that you have the insight and power to pause the default and start mixing with intention. Remember: you do not need to fix yourself; you just need to notice what's there, own your mix and choose your next ingredient intentionally. #MixNotFix.

Next, we're shifting from what's inside the bottle … to how you start filling it: purposefully, intentionally and yes, joyfully!

SECTION 2
From Flat to Fizz – Reviving Joy, Celebration and Ourselves

In Life Mixology, I use the metaphor of joy being the fizz – the essential sparkle that lifts and energises our lives and our celebrations. When it's missing, things feel flat, like something vital has been drained away.

We've already seen why this happens: the relentless pace, the pressure to perform, the hidden emotional undercurrents that go unspoken. Together, these outer societal forces and our own inner patterns fuel our growing resistance to joy and our struggle to fully engage.

That's where **Celebration Alchemy** comes in.

Alchemy is about transforming something ordinary into something precious, something magical. And that's exactly what we're doing here, reviving and transforming our relationship with celebration. And, in doing so, reconnecting to joy as a felt, living force in both everyday life and the milestone moments.

This is **Celebration 2.0:** a more intentional, soulful and satisfying way to engage with and celebrate life. Where celebration is no longer about pressure or performance. Where it's not polarising or endlessly postponed. It becomes a way of being: anchored in appreciation, fuelled by joy and aligned with what truly matters.

Celly, our Spirit of Celebration, has been nudging us quietly all along, inviting us to return to joy, to ourselves and to what's most alive. To remember the Pleasure, Possibility, Purpose and Power that celebration can offer when it's an expression of truth and love.

So how do we begin to live this way?

Through five transformative shifts that change how we think about, experience, and allow celebration to support and enrich our lives. That's what comes next: the five shifts that bring celebration back to life.

Chapter 3
Joy, Shifts and Energy Flows (Oh My!) – The Yellow Brick Road to Reconnection

You probably guessed it from the title: yes, a playful nod to *The Wizard of Oz*. But there's something deeper here too. Like Dorothy, many of us head off searching for something we believe is missing – meaning, joy, connection – only to discover that the real magic wasn't at the end of the road; it was within us all along.

In Oz, the Emerald City sparkled with promise. But the true gift was in the learning, the connection and the courage they found along the way, not the destination. That's the invitation of intentional celebration: not chasing something flashy or far-off but reconnecting to the joy that's already here, just hidden beneath stress and resistance.

The five shifts we're about to explore will help you reconnect with that joy. But first, a practical checkpoint: before you can shift how you celebrate, you need to see where you're starting from.

What's Your Current Mix?

In Chapter 2, you met the Human Components Framework – the elements that make up your Inner Mix. Now let's use it as an "audit" tool to check in with what's happening inside and spot which parts of your Inner Mix are making celebration easier, and which might be (without you realising) getting in the way *(see table that follows)*.

Remember: this isn't about fixing yourself. It's #MixNotFix – knowing yourself well enough to shift things with clarity and care. When you understand your mix, you can choose your response. And when that happens, celebration stops feeling so difficult.

How to use the table ahead:

Think about how you usually show up around moments of joy, appreciation or meaning. Then scan each row and ask yourself:

> → Right now, which state am I in? Am I operating from EGO (protecting, proving, pushing through) or SOUL FLOW (open, present, connected)?

> → What's my default pattern? Do I tend to brace for disappointment, scan for what's wrong or allow myself to savour what's good?

> → What would shift if I mixed differently? What's one small internal adjustment that would open more space for authentic celebration?

This isn't about getting it "right." It's about noticing where you are so you can choose where you want to go.

Human Component	What It Represents	EGO (How it can Inhibit Celebration)	SOUL FLOW (How it can Expand Celebration)
Personality	Core Identity in action	Stuck in conditioning. Celebrates out of habit or obligation.	Expresses authentic self. Celebration feels natural, meaningful and aligned.
Mindset	Lens on life and challenges, our perspective	Fixed or fear-based. Problem and limitations focus. Sees celebration as trivial, indulgent, undeserved or burdensome.	Growth-oriented and open. Sees possibility and joy everywhere. Celebration feels meaningful and enriching.
Beliefs and Perception	Inner stories influencing our viewpoint and experience	Limiting beliefs like *"I don't deserve this"* narrow our lens, we downplay wins and avoid joy.	*"Joy is my birthright."* Appreciation expands and honours achievements and progress.
Thinking Self	Mental chatter and inner dialogue	Overthinks, second-guesses, dismisses joy. Stuck in judgement or distracted by busyness.	Focuses intentionally on positive experiences of appreciation, meaning and joy.
Emotions	Inner compass for decisions	Suppresses or avoids emotions. Celebration feels forced or inauthentic or out of reach.	Emotions welcomed and expressed. Fuel for abundance, connection and wellbeing.
Feelings	Deeper, ongoing emotional currents	Over-identifies with stress, fear, doubt. Heaviness blocks joy and worthiness.	Grounded in peace, self-worth. Creates space for meaningful celebration.
Mood	Emotional vibe we bring	Tense, withdrawn, heavy. Spreads negativity and drains joy.	Light, open, uplifting. Spills joy and invites bonding and celebration.
Behaviours and Habits	Daily actions and patterns	On autopilot. Rarely pauses to acknowledge or appreciate. Celebration drains.	Aligned with joyful intention. Practices appreciation and gratitude. Celebration nurtures.

Now that you've seen how your inner world influences your experience of celebration, let's acknowledge the bigger picture: our cultural conditioning. We've been taught that celebration is a reward to be earned, a performance to perfect or something to save for later. No wonder it can feel awkward, indulgent or out of reach.

Here's the good news: while you can't change society overnight, you can change how you respond to it. You can choose differently, starting now.

The five shifts ahead will help you do exactly that – moving from Celebration 1.0's pressure and performance to Celebration 2.0's presence and joy. These aren't just mindset tweaks; they're transformative reframes that change how you think about, experience and allow celebration to enrich your life.

The Five Shifts

Shift 1:

Celebration isn't a luxury; it's a necessity for life, connection and resilience.

Shift 2:

Celebration isn't meaningful without intention.

Shift 3:

Celebration isn't just about achievement; it's about alignment and integration.

Shift 4:

You don't have to feel joyful to celebrate; celebration creates joy.

Shift 5:

Celebration isn't genuine without appreciation as its foundation.

Shift 1: Celebration Isn't a Luxury – It's a Necessity for Life, Connection and Resilience

We've been sold one of the biggest myths about celebration: that it's an optional indulgence – a luxury. It's so deeply ingrained that we often don't see how it holds us back from giving ourselves permission to feel joy, honour what matters and stay connected – especially when we need it most.

We know celebration once formed the bedrock of family and community life – shared rituals that marked belonging and honoured life's thresholds. Somewhere along the way, we've traded communal depth for surface celebration.

When we treat celebration as a nice-to-have – something to indulge in only when there's enough time, energy, money or reason – we cut ourselves off from the very fuel we need to revive us.

And science confirms celebration is anything but optional. Earlier, I mentioned that modern research in neuroscience and positive psychology confirms it as a powerful well-being practice that fuels resilience, belonging and connection. Without it, we burn out and lose not just joy but meaning.

We can reclaim it by remembering its purpose – to connect, to honour, to renew – and by restoring intentional celebration as part of our collective fabric, our shared legacy.

How Celebration Rewires Us for Joy

Celebration literally changes the brain. It activates the reward centres that release dopamine and oxytocin – chemistry that deepens joy, strengthens social bonds and builds resilience. Barbara Fredrickson's Broaden-and-Build Theory explains why: positive emotions expand our thinking, open us to opportunity and support long-term well-being.

Research on recognition and goal-setting echoes this – acknowledging progress, even small wins, boosts motivation, reduces stress and strengthens psychological safety at work and beyond.

Earlier, we used the SCARF model to explore how celebration can trigger a threat reaction. Now we're flipping the lens to look at the reward response. Intentional celebration and appreciation can positively activate all five domains, replenishing our sense of safety, connection and well-being.

Here's how both responses play out at a glance:

SCARF Domain	Why EGO Resists Celebration	How Celebration Replenishes
Status	Fear of standing out or being judged	Affirms self-worth and shared recognition
Certainty	Fear of jinxing success or discomfort about the unknown	Provides emotional stability and clarity through ritual and progress marking
Autonomy	Fear of being forced or losing control	Allows self-directed expression and respects choice
Relatedness	Fear of exclusion or past social wounds and stories	Builds trust, bonding and connection through shared experiences
Fairness	Fear of unfairness to others or exclusion	Normalises inclusive recognition, appreciation and shared joy

How Joy and Celebration Replenish Us

The evidence is clear: joy isn't indulgent or a luxury – it's essential. When we move out of default mode, celebration becomes a rebalancing force that restores meaning, energy and connection. Here's how the wider body of research aligns with each SCARF domain.

What the research says

- ❖ Regular acknowledgement and self-recognition strengthen intrinsic motivation and a felt sense of value (Status).

- ❖ Simple rituals reduce anxiety and create a sense of safety (Certainty).

- ❖ Self-directed, values-aligned celebration supports authenticity and well-being (Autonomy).

❖ Actively celebrating others' wins strengthens relationships more than merely offering support in tough times (Relatedness).

❖ Inclusive recognition builds cohesion and psychological safety (Fairness).

Insights to Action

The research is compelling, but insight without action doesn't change anything. Here are some practical experiments to try.

→ A rotating shout-out to acknowledge effort and results at home or at work (Status).

→ An evening reflection on three small wins to anchor progress (Certainty).

→ A quiet, self-chosen ritual to honour your way, like a solo walk or a short retreat (Autonomy).

→ A standing date in your diary for unhurried connection with family or friends, even a simple walk or shared meal (Relatedness).

→ A simple round-robin at meetings or small gatherings so everyone gets airtime and recognition (Fairness).

The Proof Is in the Joy

One of the clearest reminders of why celebration is essential came during my very first wedding as a celebrant for my dear friends, Pinky and Artur. They came to me in the midst of wedding planning overwhelm. There was a lot to navigate: different cultural backgrounds, the reality of saving for a home, families living in different countries who hadn't yet met. Choosing between Poland and England as the wedding location brought its own set of challenges and logistics.

We began working together. It wasn't a typical coaching setup. We used my intentional design process, part alchemy and part practical clarity. We got clear on what the couple truly wanted and what most mattered to them. Over six weeks, we carved out space to dream, reflect and co-create a ceremony that felt deeply true, rooted in love, meaning and shared values. We navigated stress, tension and challenges, and that vulnerability deepened bonds. What unfolded was one of the most magical and meaningful weddings I've ever witnessed.

The ceremony became the soul of the celebration, an anchoring moment, a shared spirit of joy and open-heartedness that set the tone for everything that followed. Around it, they created a magical celebration that reflected their essence as a couple. It wove together families, friends and strangers, creating new bonds and joyful connections. The ripple was tangible: warmth, wonder and the sense that something truly special had taken place. That energy lingers long after the celebration.

For me, it was living proof that when we move through resistance and show up with intention, celebration becomes transformational. If they had given in to the pressure or postponed the celebration until "the right time," they – and everyone there – would have missed out on something unforgettable and life-enriching.

This was not just a "wedding." It was a bold declaration of love, a celebration of their shared life and a healing, energising launchpad into their future. It reconnected old pals, created new friendships and raised the emotional heartbeat of everyone involved. And yes, there was fear: fear of standing out, of doing things differently, of being "too much." They chose to honour joy and love anyway. That is what celebration, at its best, can do. It doesn't just acknowledge a moment. It transforms it.

Shift 2: Celebration Isn't Meaningful Without Intention

Celebration becomes meaningful and transformative when it's intentional. Intention brings clarity to our choices – how we show up, how we engage with life and how we connect with others. Without it, celebration slips into autopilot.

Distraction fuels much of the modern celebration crisis. It's easy to be swept up by habits and pressure – scrolling, binge-watching, racing from one thing to the next. This constant motion drains our focus and energy and dulls our sense of purpose.

Intentional celebration breaks that cycle. It returns us to presence and reminds us of what truly matters.

Are we bringing baggage, operating from EGO – swept up in RAVE or stuck in FUNK – or are we arriving anchored in SOUL FLOW? When we release expectation-driven celebration and act from intention, we create experiences that carry genuine joy and resonance, rippling through our lives and relationships.

Intention is the bedrock of my celebration practice. It guides and supports me as I hold space for others in life's most sacred, joyful and sometimes heart-wrenching moments.

I learned this first through someone I admired deeply: my beloved uncle, Father Brendan. A priest and a missionary, yes – but also a philosopher, a poet and a lover of nature. Brendan radiated openness, curiosity, spiritual strength and joy that infused everything he did.

He was the embodiment of intention in action. He led most of our extended family's ceremonies – weddings, baptisms and funerals – and brought a profound sense of depth and meaning to each one. His signature was rich symbolism, but it wasn't only the outward gestures. It was the unseen care. The energy he carried, his mindset, his spiritual preparation. You could feel it. His presence changed a space.

He guided us through some of our hardest losses: my darling sister-in-law, Eileen, and my beloved eldest brother, John, both taken far too soon. Through the way he held the ceremony, we found a path through the raw grief. He helped us honour their lives with a reverence that softened the darkness.

He brought the same depth to our brighter days. Those joyful ceremonies moved us not because they were grand, but because they were personal and deeply meaningful. They had intention and love poured into them all the way through.

Long before I knew I would walk this path, he showed me that true celebration goes beneath the surface. It reaches into meaning, energy, presence and care. He was – and always will be – my greatest teacher in what it means to lead from spirit and to hold space with presence, care and deep intention.

Shift 3: Celebration Isn't Just About Achievement; It's About Alignment and Integration

We have been conditioned to celebrate the end result – the win, the milestone, the goal achieved. Real celebration goes deeper. It's about who you've become and what truly matters to you.

That's alignment and integration: honouring not just what you accomplished, but who you're becoming in the process. It's acknowledging growth, aligning with your values and bringing all parts of yourself into a more authentic whole. It brings you home to SOUL FLOW.

When we celebrate mindfully, we recognise both the outcome and the journey. I learned this in New Zealand through an experience that, on the surface, looked like failure.

I had planned a retreat with my dear friend Anne, then living in London. Pre-Zoom, we coordinated everything over Skype, dreaming, designing, preparing. As the person on the ground, I'd optimistically taken on finding attendees. But as the date drew near, there were still no sign-ups.

The external goal – a full retreat – had failed. My EGO rushed to label it all a waste, dismissing the care, effort and intention we'd poured into the programme.

But here's where alignment stepped in. At its heart, the retreat wasn't really about numbers. It was about creating meaningful connection, spiritual nourishment and intentional space – values that mattered deeply to both of us. Those values hadn't failed. They were still alive, still true.

So, we chose differently. Anne, my partner Chun Ti and I ran the retreat anyway – for ourselves. We moved through every session we'd designed. We reflected, celebrated and nourished ourselves spiritually, emotionally and physically.

That's integration: instead of splitting off the "failed" part (no attendees) from the "successful" part (our intention and care), we brought it all together. We honoured what we'd built and what we'd learned. We acknowledged the disappointment and the gift. We held the tension of both, and in doing so, found something whole.

Letting go of the external measures revealed a deeper truth. The retreat's value wasn't in how many people showed up. It was in how aligned we stayed with what mattered to us, and how fully we integrated the entire experience – including the disappointment – into something meaningful.

When celebration is grounded in SOUL, it's always valuable. Even when it may not look like a success.

Shift 4: You Don't Have to Feel Joyful to Celebrate – Celebration Creates Joy

We often assume we need to be happy or "in the mood" to celebrate. But the act of celebration itself cultivates joy. When we acknowledge and honour a moment, however small or heavy, we open the door to joy – even when it wasn't there before.

I have fully lived this shift. It did not come from theory or research; it came from life, from the raw, real moments when joy felt out of reach and celebration led the way back.

I love Christmas. But in recent years, grief made everything heavy. Too many Christmases were marked by devastating loss – a first Christmas without someone we loved, and heartbreakingly, a last Christmas with another, without knowing it.

In the midst of it all, celebration felt like the last thing anyone wanted. But I intuitively knew we needed to celebrate anyway. Each year, I created the Christmas cheer and we showed up for each other, lit candles, set the table, honoured the moment together – even through the heaviness.

Those memories of last Christmases are now among our most cherished.

My milestone birthday fell in another season of grief. I was in no place to plan a party or want to call attention to myself. But when family and friends offered to celebrate, I remembered: I don't just teach this work, I believe in it.

I said yes, even through the grief. And everything softened. From those celebrations came fresh energy and creativity – some of which became this book.

This is why this shift matters so deeply to me. Celebration has the power to carry us forward, even when we are weary or grief-stricken. If you're still not convinced, let me share the story of my darling youngest brother, Brendie.

We had planned our first-ever siblings' family holiday. A few weeks before, Brendie had what we thought was a tummy bug. Days before the holiday, we got the devastating news that he was terminal – six months at most. We went on holiday anyway, a precious week.

When we returned, he was weaker. But it was his birthday week, and there was nothing Brendie liked more than dressing up and having a party. So, we celebrated – many times over – even though we were tired, emotional and reeling from what felt impossible. We put our best foot, and face, forward for him. Even as he grew sicker by the day, he lifted everyone up around him.

A few days later, he was gone.

He reinforced this shift in the most powerful way imaginable: you don't have to feel joyful to celebrate; through celebration, joy finds you. That joy – our shared "haka" (I'll explain later), his beaming smile, the delight in being celebrated and photographed! – now brings deep and lasting comfort.

Celebration is not optional or indulgent. It's an intentional act of honouring what's precious. And when we do that – when we show up anyway – joy follows. It may be quiet, it may be gentle, but it helps. It heals. It gives hope. In our case, it gave us precious memories to keep our hearts warm in the cold, dark cave of shock and grief.

When Intention Matters More Than Motivation

We often wait to feel like doing something before we act. Especially when it comes to celebration, we assume we need to be in the "right" emotional state first. But waiting for motivation can leave us stuck in the heaviness. That's why intention becomes your way forward when motivation is lacking.

Motivation is tied to emotional energy; it's how much drive we feel in a given moment. And when we're running on empty, caught in stress, grief, distraction, or overwhelm, it's often the first thing that deserts us.

Intention is different. Intention is your compass. It doesn't depend on mood or energy. It comes from something deeper: your values, your vision and your sense of purpose. Think of motivation as the fuel in your tank; it gets you going, but it runs out. Intention is your internal GPS; even if the tank is low, your direction stays clear.

That is the power of intentional celebration. You may not feel like showing up, but what matters to you can carry you forward. The act of honouring a moment – however small – can be the starting point. Once you begin, momentum builds, and joy starts to return. You don't have to wait for motivation. You can choose intention and let celebration create the joy.

Shift 5: Celebration Isn't Genuine Without Appreciation as Its Foundation

Appreciation is the foundation of true celebration; it's what keeps it genuine. It anchors us in the moment, helps us notice the good and brings joy and gratitude. Appreciation and celebration feed each other. The more you acknowledge what's good, the more you find to celebrate. And the more you celebrate, the more attuned you become to what deserves appreciation.

If celebration is the fire, appreciation is the spark that ignites it. It's how we reclaim joy in the moment, not by waiting for something extraordinary to happen, but by noticing what's already good in our lives.

The word *appreciation* comes from the Latin *appretiatus,* meaning "to value highly" or "to give something weight." It's also the same root as the financial term: when something appreciates, its worth grows. Similarly, when we appreciate the moments of our lives and celebrate them, they grow in value and meaning. Life feels richer and more precious because we took time to notice.

We've seen that in our default mode, we skim past the good; positive experiences slide off like Teflon, while negative ones stick like Velcro. Appreciation interrupts autopilot and slows us down, letting the good sink in. It helps us see the significance in everyday beauty and small, meaningful moments, not just the big milestones or grand gestures. We recognise the extraordinary in the ordinary. It's where my go-to mantra and mission of #MakingMomentsMatter comes from.

Appreciation isn't only about the external. Self-appreciation is a crucial, often overlooked part of the mix. It begins with valuing your own efforts, your growth, your resilience and recognising that your journey matters. The more we acknowledge the good in ourselves, the more good we begin to see.

Dr Masaru Emoto's work with water crystals offers a compelling metaphor: when water was exposed to loving words, it formed beautiful crystalline patterns. Harsh words created chaos. Whether you take this literally or as metaphor, the principle holds: the language we use – especially with ourselves – has power.

And remember: the human body is around 60 per cent water. Our internal dialogue matters. How we speak to ourselves has the power to uplift and expand or diminish and contract us.

What if, instead of criticism or judgement, we offered ourselves kindness and appreciation? What if we used *"look how far I've come"* instead of *"not good enough"*? Small internal shifts can have a profound effect, not only on how we feel, but on how we engage with and experience life.

This is the foundation of self-celebration – a practice that goes beyond vision boards or goal-setting. Neuroscience backs this up: when you operate from self-criticism and shame, your nervous system stays in threat mode. Your brain is wired for survival, not growth. But self-appreciation activates different neural pathways – ones associated with safety, openness and possibility.

You can set all the intentions in the world, but without self-acceptance as your base, your nervous system won't let you receive the good. You're trying to build dreams while your body is braced for danger. Self-appreciation isn't self-indulgence. It's the neurological foundation that makes transformation possible.

You might wonder what self-appreciation looks like in real life. Well, in our family, it sounds something like this: *"C'mon, myself!"*

My mum was from a small island called Whiddy in West Cork, Ireland. She was a champion rower and a popular girl. At every regatta, she had boisterous supporters. One race day, a competitor had no one in the crowd cheering for her. Meanwhile, the shouts for my mum kept growing louder: "C'mon, Kathleen!" "C'mon, Kathleen!" Then, something beautiful happened. That girl, rowing with all her might, started cheering for herself. As she pulled the oars, she kept shouting, "C'mon, myself! C'mon, myself!"

Our family adopted that phrase as a kind of personal mantra – a self-encouraging pat on the back. We've even blended it with our beloved brother Brendie's "haka." Brendie was non-verbal, but his haka was unmistakable: thunderous applause followed by both arms thrust up repeatedly in victory. It's become a meaningful family ritual, lifting our spirits every time, as we laugh and recall cherished memories. That story and Brendie's haka have now travelled far and wide, and that feels very special.

I invite you to create your own version. Let it be your foundation.

Each of the five shifts opens a different door to the same transformation: from surviving to flourishing, from flatness to fizz. They help you rethink what celebration really is, how it works, and why it matters, especially in a world that pulls us into pressure, performance and distraction.

You've seen that celebration is more than a mood; it's a mindset and a practice. That motivation isn't required when intention is present. That joy is created, not found. And that appreciation makes life more precious.

When we choose to notice, appreciate and celebrate, we reconnect with what's good and meaningful. The more we practice, the more aligned we become with what's true. We don't need to fix ourselves, chase joy, force connection or wait until we're "ready." We simply need to mix in more joy, more meaning and more intention.

That's where Life Mixology comes in. #MixNotFix.

Chapter 4
Fizz by Design – The Life Mixology Method to Reclaim Joy (and Celebration)

We ended the last chapter with an important reminder, one of my most significant personal ahas: you do not need fixing ... because you are not broken. You already have what you need to live a fulfilling, joyful life. But most of us have never been taught how to work with what's already inside us. This chapter is about learning to do just that.

Life doesn't happen around us, or to us – it happens *through* us. That insight tilted my axis. For years, I believed that if I could just get the right external circumstances, the right timing, the right version of me, then I'd be okay. I could feel good. Life would finally click into place. That belief kept me chasing and trying to control everything. I hadn't realised what was going on inside, let alone how to work with it. I was so busy putting out external fires that I'd bolted shut the door to my inner world. And the self-help world wasn't much help either, only digging me deeper into trying to "fix" what was never broken.

Eventually, I came to see the truth: it's our *inner world* that determines how we meet life, how we interpret it and ultimately, how we live it. That changed everything.

Years of distraction and disconnection gave way to a gradual unlayering. Slowly, I began to understand my own internal mix: the thoughts, beliefs, emotions and patterns that influenced my living. With this shift, I stopped trying to become "perfect" and started being the mixologist of my own experience.

I'll never forget the moment this truth finally landed in my bones. Strangely enough, it happened while watching a boxing movie, a genre I usually avoid. But something drew me to watch. It was a biopic about the legendary George Foreman, and at the end, he said something that sent shivers down my spine. One sentence cut straight to my core; I paused and rewatched and then transcribed it:

> *"I had to get knocked down to the very bottom, to finally see that everything I was searching for was already there and with that, you can do the impossible."*

That line was a taser zap of truth. It didn't just echo what I'd been circling for years; it cracked it open.

Even though I'd looked within, I hadn't really done anything with what I'd found. Despite "knowing" differently, I was still stuck in the ingrained loop of seeking, studying, fixing, waiting for something outside me to shift.

This was the shove I needed. The realisation that I truly create my own reality. That's where my Life Mixology method was born – and my mission to bring celebration to life became crystal clear.

Like Dorothy discovering the magic was within her all along, we don't need to become someone else or wait for the "right" moment. Everything we need is already here. We just need to understand what's in our bottle, our Inner Mix, get clear on why it matters, and learn how to work with it.

That's what comes next.

What Is Life Mixology?

At its simplest, mixology is the art of crafting a cocktail; thoughtfully combining ingredients to create something that delights the senses. Life Mixology applies that same artistry to your inner world.

Life Mixology is twofold:

> **First,** it's becoming aware of your Inner Mix and identifying the key ingredients that influence how you think, feel, respond and engage. **Second,** it's understanding how those components interact: how thoughts fuel emotions, beliefs influence behaviour, mindsets drive choices and habits can either keep you aligned or pull you off track.

That's the Life Mixology method in a nutshell. In short: not fixing yourself, but appreciating what's there and experimenting with a remix. #MixNotFix

A Quick Word on Mixology

The "mixology" and cocktail metaphor came to me intuitively, but I resisted it initially. On the surface, why wouldn't I use it? As an Irishwoman with many years in the hospitality industry – who relishes a great cocktail – it was a natural fit. But then I found myself second-guessing it.

Would it seem too frivolous, or worse, reinforce that dreaded Irish stereotype about drinking? And then I realised I was doing the very thing I guide others to move through: rejecting a joyful, aligned idea because of fear of judgement. *(Mutter, mutter.)* So, here we are. Mixology it is. Playful, practical and, yes, mocktails included.

Life Mixology 101: Understanding the Basics

In Chapter 2, we uncorked your bottle and explored your Inner Mix: your two operating states (EGO and SOUL), your Shadow, the four levels of consciousness, and your core components (e.g. mindset, beliefs, habits, emotions). That's Life Mixology 101 – understanding what's inside.

Now comes the question: what do we do with this knowledge?

We have a choice. We can keep juggling, reacting and trying to control everything life throws at us – feeling increasingly drained and powerless. Or we can take the wheel and choose our direction, live life our way, on purpose. That's what I call "applied mixology": consciously moving from managing life to crafting it.

Life Mixology 1.0: The Default Recipe

The automatic processing of the subconscious can make life run more efficiently. But it also pulls us onto autopilot, repeating old patterns without realising it. Like the frog in the pot, we often don't notice how uncomfortable life has become until we're already burnt out.

This is Life Mixology 1.0: living by default. Left unchecked, our inner mix runs on survival scripts, conditioning and egoic habits. It's a recipe we never consciously chose, handed to us by EGO, blended by conditioning, flavoured with fatigue, fear or habit. A concoction of proving, pleasing, avoiding and overdoing.

Remember those EGO modes from Chapter 2? In Life Mixology 1.0, they become your default settings: swinging between RAVE (reactive, agitated, validation-seeking, escaping) and FUNK (fearful, unmotivated, numb, keeping small). Neither mode fuels joy, and the constant swing between them is exhausting.

It's like drinking from the same old bottle – a pre-mixed cocktail that's sometimes sickly sweet, sometimes sharply bitter, but rarely satisfying. This is our modern-day celebration crisis: Celebration 1.0, where we're distracted and disconnected from joy, aliveness and each other.

Life Mixology 1.0 The EGO bottle - pressurised, unsettled, stuck in Celebration 1.0.

Life Mixology 2.0: Your Conscious Mix

There's another way forward: more intentional, energising and aligned. Enter: Life Mixology 2.0. This shift begins when we wake up, become more self-aware and reclaim our power. We begin to choose how we want to operate, how we want to experience life and how we want others to experience us.

By setting the intention to live from our SOUL state, we move into FLOW: flexible, light, optimistic, willing. It's like pouring from a fresh, handcrafted mix – balanced, vibrant and uniquely yours. In FLOW, it overflows with joy, connection and wholehearted presence.

Life Mixology 2.0 The SOUL bottle - balanced, vibrant, flowing with Celebration 2.0.

This is you bringing your unique blend of intention, energy and values into everyday life. This is what brings celebration to life, not as an afterthought or obligation, but as a mindset and practice that enriches and enlivens. This is living the new paradigm of Celebration 2.0.

Life Mixology as a Lived Experience

Of course, we all slip between these two states. That's part of being human. In fact, we need to experience both; we'll explore this later as "Creative Tension." The key is noticing and choosing again. Learning to mix with purpose, curiosity, patience and compassion. #MixNotFix

So what does remixing your inner state actually look like?

It might mean shifting from a fixed mindset (*I'm just not good at this*) to a growth one (*I'm learning, and that's enough*). Or catching yourself stuck in negativity or comparison and gently steering your attention back to what's appreciable in the moment. Or recognising when old survival habits kick in and choosing, even in small ways, to bring more curiosity, compassion or lightness into the mix.

Remember: EGO and SOUL operate like a switch – you can't run both at once. These small, conscious choices are how you flip the switch. This is Life Mixology 2.0 in action.

The Journey from 1.0 to 2.0

When life feels messy, heavy or uncertain, our old survival scripts kick in, trying to keep us safe. But they often make things worse – defending in ways that create more tension, more pressure, more disconnection. Ego rushes to fix what feels broken. But pouring energy into fixing only keeps us stuck. As Dan Millman writes in *The Way of the Peaceful Warrior*:

> *"The secret of change is to focus all your energy not on fighting the old, but on building the new."*

When we intentionally shift our internal settings – choosing SOUL over EGO, presence over pressure – we create something new. *That's the transformative magic of Life Mixology.*

The bridge that carries us from 1.0 to 2.0 is powered by three simple but profound tools – I call them our "hidden superpowers":

→ **Intention:** Your compass. It gives direction to your energy and choices.

→ **Attention:** Your spotlight. It determines what gets your focus.

→ **Noticing:** Your quiet lens. It reveals what's already here waiting.

In Life Mixology 1.0, these powers are often hijacked: *intention* gets lost to people-pleasing or perfectionism; *attention* is caught up in threat-scanning; and *noticing* turns passive, blind to beauty, joy or possibility.

In Life Mixology 2.0, *intention* becomes a grounding force that guides us towards what matters to us. *Attention* shifts to what lifts and connects us. *Noticing* comes alive, helping us savour the meaning in the moment.

Here's what this looks like: You wake up feeling really anxious about your day. *Intention:* You choose to approach the day with curiosity, not dread. *Attention:* You shift from the mental to-do list to the warmth of your coffee, the morning light. *Noticing:* You catch yourself smiling at something small – and let yourself feel it. The day hasn't changed, but your energy has.

That's how simple these shifts can be. Once you set your *intention*, *attention* and *noticing* almost happen automatically. You just need to remember to use them.

Together, they shift our perception, build new patterns and help us experience more presence, appreciation and joy.

How Small Changes Create Big Shifts

Ever noticed that once you start thinking of a particular thing, say red cars, you suddenly see them everywhere? That's your brain's filter at work, highlighting what you're focused on.

The same principle applies to joy and appreciation. Each time you genuinely notice something good, your brain's filter highlights more of it. Life hasn't changed, but your experience of it has. That's neuroplasticity in action. Every small moment of appreciation lays down a new track in your subconscious.

As Lao Tzu said:

> *"Watch your thoughts; they become your words.*
> *Watch your words; they become your actions.*
> *Watch your actions; they become your habits.*
> *Watch your habits; they become your character.*
> *Watch your character; it becomes your destiny."*

One small pebble dropped in the pond of your subconscious sends ripples. That's how transformation begins, quietly, gradually, powerfully. You start reinforcing a new story. One that says: *There is joy here. This moment matters. And so do I.*

Practicing Appreciation

I didn't always appreciate the power of appreciation. But a funny (and slightly messy) real-life moment planted the seed for one of my most transformative practices.

My extraordinary parents had just touched down in New Zealand – their first visit, after flying all the way from Ireland without a layover – to see my partner and me. What began as a simple welcome drink became a favourite memory of my late folks and my beloved Chun Ti together.

We were standing around, drinks poured (no jetlag excuses with my oldies!), when my usually reserved mum turned to Chun Ti mid-toast and said, "Oh, you can't toast without catching each other's eyes." Then she added, deadpan, "Otherwise, it means seven years of bad sex."

Chun Ti, mid-sip, choked and sprayed his drink all over us. We laughed until we cried. That playful practice – the exaggerated eye contact every time we raised a glass – became a ritual that lives on with family and friends. Because it wasn't just fun; it anchored something deeper: connection, presence and shared joy.

That ritual inspired me to begin noticing and appreciating the power of small, beautiful moments in my life. It got me thinking: *How could I intentionally anchor this energy of joy, love, humour and connection in everyday life, not just during celebrations?*

Over time, that reflection led to the creation of my CHEERS touchstone – a simple cue to pause, appreciate and make a moment matter. Here's what it stands for:

⟋ **CHEERS™**

    C: Choose to

    H: Honour the moment

    E: Embrace it

    E: Engage with it

    R: Reflect

    S: Savour (and Share)

You'll find CHEERS in more detail in Chapter 7.

You Get to Choose

The reason a touchstone like CHEERS can help rewire your brain and reclaim joy is that it taps into the engine of change – your three hidden superpowers that carry you from Life Mixology 1.0 to 2.0:

→ We set an intention

→ We focus our attention

→ We notice the beauty already here

These simple choices are how we begin to mix a life worth celebrating, from the inside out.

Mixing Your Inner World for Outer Magic

You now understand your Inner Mix – the operating states, patterns and components that shape your experience. You've met your three super-powers: intention, attention, noticing. You know the difference between autopilot pre-mix (1.0) and mixing with purpose (2.0).

Now it's time to bring this understanding to life through celebration. We'll use two metaphors from mixology to connect your inner state with your outer presence:

- ❖ Your Inner Mix as cocktails: your **Signature Mix** (your baseline inner blend) and your **Celebration Cocktail** (how that blend shifts when you're preparing to celebrate with others).

- ❖ Your **Glass** as your capacity to hold and savour joy.

These aren't just abstract concepts. They're practical tools for understanding why some celebrations feel energising while others drain you, why you might show up one way at family gatherings and another at work events and how to consciously choose the energy you bring.

Let's start with your Inner Mix.

Your Signature Mix™

Through Life Mixology, you've seen how your Inner Mix affects everything: your energy, your presence, your impact. Your Signature Mix is this inner blend at its most essential – it's you when no one's around, the baseline that colours how you experience life. And we've seen how the flavour changes depending on your operating state: EGO pre-mix in Life Mixology 1.0, or SOUL FLOW crafting in Life Mixology 2.0.

Your Signature Mix: It's you, when no one's around – the inner blend that colours how you experience life.

Your Inner Mix is uniquely yours. You're discovering what ingredients fuel you and keep you aligned, or what flattens you. There is no right or wrong way to #MixNotFix. This is you becoming a master mixologist. You're learning to mix with awareness, so what's inside supports how you want to show up outside.

In the next section, you'll discover how your Signature Mix shifts and evolves into your **Celebration Cocktail** when you're preparing to celebrate with others. That's where Life Mixology becomes the foundation for Celebration Alchemy. It's where you'll learn to work with your mix in real time, moving from theory to practice, from insight to experiment.

Your Glass

While your Signature Mix reflects your energetic flavour, your Glass represents your current capacity to receive and savour joy. Even the most exquisite cocktail loses its magic if the glass is too small, cracked or leaking.

How do you strengthen your glass? By living the principles we've been exploring: noticing what's good, appreciating what matters, celebrating what's here. These aren't just feel-good practices – they're the foundation of well-being. The more you practice them, the more your capacity expands. Your glass gets bigger, stronger, more resilient.

Celebration does this naturally. When you celebrate, you're actively building your capacity for joy. You're training your brain to notice the good, strengthening your relationships, creating meaning and honouring what you've accomplished. Celebration doesn't just fill your glass – it makes the glass itself more able to hold joy.

Celebration is the powerhouse of your Life Mixology lab.

#FizzByDesign is our shorthand for you, the master mixologist, crafting your life with intention. Mixing isn't once-and-done. Life doesn't work that way. To be a mixologist is to keep experimenting: with curiosity, intention, patience and the willingness to try new flavours. And the best place to start? Celebration.

We've seen how it reveals what's been missing or misaligned, how auto-pilot has taken over and how pressure and expectations have crowded out joy. Too often, what we've called "celebration" has been about appearance and performance, and that's why it's fallen flat.

But when we mix differently – with intention instead of autopilot – everything changes. That's the essence of Celebration 2.0: celebration as remedy, rebalancing and a new way of relating to life. It becomes a living, breathing practice, a way to try out new blends of mindset, emotion and energy. You keep what nourishes. You let go of what doesn't. You keep mixing. You keep learning.

And it's not just about planning parties or marking milestones. It's about how you move through your days, how you notice what matters, connect with who you are and savour what's already here. Celebration becomes a way of living, personally and collectively.

SECTION 3
Celebration 2.0 and
The Spirit of Celebration

Life Mixology matters because it's how we bring Celebration 2.0 to life. You've uncorked your bottle. You understand your Inner Mix – the operating states, patterns and beliefs that shape your experience. You know the difference between mixing on autopilot (1.0) and mixing with purpose (2.0). You have your three superpowers: intention, attention, noticing.

Now comes the practice: tending to your Inner Mix with presence, appreciation and heart. Choosing to live more intentionally. To reconnect that part of you that has always known how to savour, to create, to celebrate.

You'll discover how your Inner Mix evolves into your Celebration Cocktail – the unique energy you bring when celebrating with others – and learn to strengthen your Glass, your capacity to hold and savour joy.

This is where your inner work flows into how you show up – for yourself, for others and for the moments that matter.

Because at its core, this work isn't just about understanding yourself – it's about expressing spirit, joy and love through celebration.

What's Ahead

You'll meet Celly, **the Spirit of Celebration** – a guide, a companion, a reminder that joy has always been here, waiting to be welcomed back in.

You'll discover **Celebration Alchemy** – the art of transforming ordinary moments into meaning, connection and magic. Not through perfection or performance, but through presence, appreciation and intention.

And you'll explore **Co-Celebration** – the shift from being a guest to being a participant. From waiting for joy to creating it. From celebrating alone to catalysing celebration in community.

This is about reclaiming celebration as a practice that strengthens relationships, honours what matters and recharges our collective spirit. It's about returning to what celebration was always meant to be: a way of living that says yes to life, even when life is messy.

Welcome to Celebration 2.0.

Chapter 5
Celebration Alchemy – The Art of Stirring Magic and Spilling Joy

When most people think about celebration, they picture parties, milestones, or big moments: birthdays, weddings, clinking glasses, posed photos. We've been conditioned to see celebration as something external: something we do, somewhere we go, reserved for special occasions and organised events. More and more, it becomes just another pressure point.

But that's not all celebration is, or can be.

True celebration goes deeper. It's a way of being: how we notice the good, how we connect with others, how we stay open to meaning in the smallest, most ordinary moments. It's a spirit and energy we can invite into everyday life, whenever we choose.

This is Celebration 2.0. A reset in how we see, feel and relate to celebration. Not as an occasional treat, but as a vital and nourishing part of being alive. A practice for the individual, a culture for the collective, brought to life through Celebration Alchemy.

The more we give to it, the more it gives back. It deepens our joy, strengthens our relationships and enriches our communities. This is the path Celly invites us towards: not a celebration of successes alone, but a celebration of life itself. One breath, one moment, one heartfelt offering at a time.

Celebration 2.0 - a new paradigm grounded in joy, connection and shared humanity. Guided by the Spirit of Celebration.

The Spirit of Celebration

Initially, I revered the Spirit of Celebration as a kind of high priestess: sacred, spiritual and hushed, like being in church on a Sunday. You approached with care and reverence, and only on special occasions. There was always a lot of preparation: scrubbed up, best clothes on, behaviour adjusted. That began to change as I grew into my role as a celebrant. The Spirit no longer felt like something outside of me.

I learned to tap into her energy to serve others, to bring meaning, presence and connection to milestone moments. But I still hadn't seen her as my personal guide. Then came my "George Foreman" moment, a quiet, complete shift in my inner axis. That was when my relationship with her deepened and she became *Celly*. I stopped admiring her from a distance and embraced her, not only as an energy to call on, but as a companion – a playful guide who nourished my soul and reminded me how to feel alive. I felt myself drawn to dancing on the lawn at dawn, grounded in the morning dew. Slowing down to notice life, reflecting and appreciating the moments and the people.

Celly is not loud, just quietly present in the silence, the laughter and the tears. Maybe you've already sensed her in fleeting moments: in the warmth of connection, the tinkle of shared laughter, the soft exhale after a long day. She is not about pretence or performance. She's an invitation to come home, to remember what matters and to honour what is here. She shows up when you allow joy to land without apology and when you support others with love. The Spirit of Celebration does not ask for much, only that we remember she is here, waiting to be welcomed in.

Celebration Alchemy 101

Celebration Alchemy is working with celebration as a living force. Not just something to plan, but something to co-create. It is about relationships: with yourself and your values, with your people, and with joy itself.

You do this by using your energy, attention and intention to let meaning, magic and connection emerge. You're recognising that joy is not something to chase or earn or find outside ourselves. It's something we can tend to, like an ember that's waiting for breath and kindling to spark it back to life.

Why "Alchemy?"

Alchemy is the art of transformation. An ancient practice, rich with the wisdom and curiosity of the ages. We know it for turning lead into gold; the true magic behind this lies in working with what is – seen and unseen – and masterfully crafting it into something more. Transforming the ordinary into the extraordinary.

That is why it feels so true and aligned to bring it into our celebration journey. Celebration Alchemy is more than organising or commemorating. It is *bringing celebration to life*. This works in two ways:

First, reviving celebration itself – reimagining how we mark milestones and special occasions.

Second, weaving celebration into the everyday – the pauses and the small rituals of appreciation that add meaning to our lives.

At the heart of this practice is our connection with Celly. She reminds us that true celebration is available anytime. Celebration Alchemy re-energises this connection, creating space for joy, meaning, shared magic and pleasure. As you begin to live this way, you shift the vibe. You feel the difference, and the people around you sense it too.

Celly, the Spirit of Celebration - *a soulful presence and dynamic force that fuels Celebration 2.0.*

Five Core Elements of Celebration 2.0

Earlier, we explored five key shifts that address our celebration crisis: celebration that's more stressful than joyful, more performance than presence, more pressure than pleasure. These shifts reframe celebration as essential, intentional and deeply meaningful. (See recap box).

The Five Shifts that Bring Celebration 2.0 to Life

Shift 1:

Celebration isn't a luxury; it's a necessity for life, connection and resilience.

Shift 2:

Celebration isn't meaningful without intention.

Shift 3:

Celebration isn't just about achievement; it's about alignment and integration.

Shift 4:

You don't have to feel joyful to celebrate; celebration creates joy.

Shift 5:

Celebration isn't genuine without appreciation as its foundation.

These shifts reveal deeper energies we've been missing. Their essence distils into five living elements that fuel Celebration 2.0 and give Celebration Alchemy its power. They're the energetic ingredients Celly draws on, and you can too.

The Five Core Elements:

- ❖ **Energy** – the life force that fuels and replenishes us (Shift 1).

- ❖ **Intention** – the guiding compass that steers our presence and choices (Shift 2).

- ❖ **Alignment** – the harmony that arises when we act in sync with our truth (Shift 3).

- ❖ **Joy** – the soul-fuel that lights us up from the inside out (Shift 4).

- ❖ **Presence** – the quality of attention that fosters appreciation (Shift 5).

You don't have to learn anything new to start. Begin by noticing these five elements in your everyday life. See when they show up, how they feel and where a little more attention could bring more joy and meaning.

Energy: Dynamic Exchange

Energy includes your overall vitality and your in-the-moment emotional and physical charge. It's our life force and our fuel. Celebration takes energy. When we're already exhausted or stressed, it drains. When we're aligned and intentional, it gives back in a two-way flow that fuels and replenishes us – a dynamic exchange.

> **Example:** You're tired. The day's been full on, and nothing feels particularly joyful. You decide to pause anyway, light a candle, put on a favourite song and high-five yourself for getting through it. You breathe, and a smile emerges. You didn't start with energy; you created it. That's the exchange: celebration, even the small, personal kind, gives back.

Intention: The Quiet Guide

Intention is your inner compass that steers your presence, focus and choices. More than a vague hope, it's a heart-led signal that says *this matters,* steadying your centre and guiding you back when you drift.

> **Example:** You want a family gathering to feel relaxed and joyful, not tense. You set an intention: to be present, not to fuss. Perfection drops away; you focus on connection and the whole tone shifts.

Alignment: Inner Harmony and Outer Flow

Alignment is the sweet spot where values, emotions, beliefs and actions are all in sync. You're not performing or pretending. You're simply showing up fully as yourself. Alignment frees energy, calms the noise and makes your presence feel steady and true.

> **Example:** Everyone expects a big milestone birthday bash. You check in and realise you want something smaller, more intimate. A space to reconnect and recharge with a few special people. You choose that, and your whole system settles. You feel more grounded, more honest, more you.

Joy: Soul-Fuel

Joy is the soul-fuel of celebration. It's what lights you up from the inside. It is felt aliveness that lifts and softens, bringing warmth to even the smallest exchange – celebration's glow. And the more you choose it, the more it shows up.

> **Example:** You're doing the dishes with your partner; the dishwasher's broken again. You're rushing and stressed, mind on work. Suddenly, dish water splashes all over your new silk blouse. You freeze. He looks at you, wide-eyed. For some reason, instead of snapping, you burst out laughing at his horrified expression. The tension breaks. Something in you lightens. Not perfect, but real. That's joy, sneaking in through the cracks (or the suds), reminding you that life doesn't have to be a frantic rush; that joy can be a simple moment, shared.

Presence: #MakingMomentsMatter

Presence is showing up fully, giving your attention, energy and care to what's happening right now. It's choosing not to rush through or be half-there. It turns the fleeting into the appreciated and helps others feel safe, seen and connected.

> **Example:** Work is frantic; you're stressed to the max. A small bird landing outside your window catches your eye. You notice its soft movement, the way it tilts its head, looking at you curiously. For just a moment, the noise fades; you breathe deeply, coming back to your

body. Nothing outside has changed, but you have. That's presence: the power to return to now, to beauty, to yourself, even (especially) in the middle of the mess.

Bringing It All Together

These five elements – Celebration Alchemy's lifeforce – are always at play, whether or not we notice them. They are not forces to manipulate; they are energies to observe and experiment with.

When they work in harmony, something greater emerges: **Joytality** – the alchemised state of living and celebrating with these energies alive in you.

Joytality: Cultivating *Joie de Vivre*

The word Joytality was gifted to me – one of Celly's whispers. It's a state, a feeling, a presence: the energy that flows when joy and vitality dance together through your life. Like a pulse that brightens your days, softens your edges and brings colour to even the greyest moments. It holds laughter and sorrow, love and memory, meaning and light.

Joytality isn't about being relentlessly upbeat or pretending everything's fine. It's not forced happiness or toxic positivity. It's living from your essence instead of an outdated script designed to keep you small – a return to innocence, wonder and awe. It's your soul-sourced fizz of aliveness.

I often pair it with *joie de vivre,* in a quiet tribute to a lovely senior consultant I worked with in my first job at a hospital in southern Ireland. Let's call him "HK" – a big man in every way: height, intellect, voice and presence. One lunchtime, after laughing at something I'd said, he declared, "You know, Siobhán, you're the epitome of joie de vivre."

Back then, I had to look it up, but the phrase stuck. It became a touchstone pinned on the walls of my home offices across many countries – a warm talisman I reached for on darker days when laughter felt far away. It reminded me that joy is my birthright, my fuel and my soul source. That memory is part of why *Joytality* was born. So, thank you, HK – wherever you are – you touched my heart and my life.

Joytality in Everyday Life

At its heart, Joytality is your living expression of the five elements – animating celebration and enriching the everyday. It helps you appreciate being truly alive, in the messy and the magical alike.

It appears in ordinary moments: when you pause mid-rush to notice the light and feel a quiet smile rise. When a memory nudges you to send a simple "thinking of you" message. When tension breaks and laughter spills out in the middle of chaos.

These small acts are Joytality in motion. They create a reservoir within you – refilled every time you celebrate with awareness and heart – sustaining you when life feels heavy. Joytality reminds you of who you are and what truly matters.

You Are a Celebration Alchemist

When you begin to work consciously with the five Core Elements, you're no longer just celebrating – you're becoming a **Celebration Alchemist:** part craftsman, part magician, transforming the ordinary into the extraordinary and inviting in the Spirit of Celebration.

As a Celebration Alchemist, you use life experience as your base metal. Through the Core Elements – in everyday moments or major milestones – you take what you have and mix it with meaning, presence and appreciation. You don't wait for perfect timing, the right mood or a clear schedule. The reasons to delay are endless, but delay too long and joy slips through your fingers. You create the moment. You give yourself permission to feel the joy and to celebrate fully.

I once joked that being a wedding celebrant felt like holding a *"Licence to Thrill"* – a nod to James Bond, of course – a permission slip to deliberately craft joy. Later, what rang truer was that it's more like a "Licence to Spill" – and it's one we all share.

Psychologists call it the *spillover effect:* how our inner state flows into the spaces and relationships around us. When we're aligned – living from SOUL, resourced and present – we become **SpillJoys,** people whose gratitude and appreciation overflow and lift those around them, creating moments of connection and magic.

Of course, spillover can have a less positive effect. When we're struggling under stress, it's our pain that leaks out. With compassion, we can see that what looks like someone "being a pain" is often someone in pain, coping as best they can.

Choosing to notice what we spill – and to spill joy whenever we can – keeps celebration alive in the present. Joy isn't always neat or glittering; celebration doesn't always come with champagne. Sometimes it's a quiet pause, a shared smile, a toast to someone who isn't there. It's the golden thread we weave through our lives and the lives of those we love.

This is what it means to be a Celebration Alchemist.

How Your Inner Mix Shows Up In Celebration

Let's return to the cocktail metaphor from Chapter 4. You've started exploring your **Signature Mix** – your baseline inner blend, the unique cocktail that's just you when you're alone.

Remember when I said that blend shifts when you're preparing to celebrate with others? Let's explore what that shift looks like – and why it matters.

When celebration enters the picture, your inner blend adapts. The core ingredients stay the same, but the proportions shift. What felt balanced in solitude might need adjusting when you're preparing to connect, to be seen, to mark a milestone. This shifted blend is your Celebration Cocktail.

Your Celebration Cocktail™

Your Signature Mix is your constant; your Celebration Cocktail is context-specific. It reflects how you intend to show up (or assume you will), and how you meet joy and meaning in real time. This Cocktail lives inside you; it flavours your presence before a word is spoken.

Your Celebration Cocktail, your inner blend – the flavour and energy you mix when you're getting ready to celebrate.

In Celebration 1.0, your Celebration Cocktail is the pre-mixed version: the default recipe, flavoured by old wounds, conditioning, limiting beliefs and a lot of "shoulds." Blended from stories of what to celebrate, how to act and what's appropriate. It's EGO behind the bar, slinging out the same tired blend of over-functioning, people-pleasing or perfectionism.

In Celebration 2.0, the experience changes. You handcraft the mix with intention and purpose. You infuse it with celebration's Core Elements. You honour your energy. You stop performing celebration and start embodying it as soul-fuel. You become conscious not only of what is in the glass, but also of its condition.

The Glass: Your Capacity to Hold Joy

Your glass is your energetic vessel. Its condition reflects your ability to receive and hold celebration, to let joy land and linger. What's happening in your inner and outer life directly impacts how full, cracked or leaky that glass feels.

> **Running on empty?** Stretched too thin or stuck in survival mode? Your glass might feel small, like there's just no room left. Stress and over-functioning can slowly shrink your capacity (remember the frog in the pot?).

Carrying old wounds or harsh self-judgement? Your glass might be cracked. Even when goodness comes in, it leaks out through the gaps of doubt, mistrust or emotional fatigue.

Constantly giving to others? If you're pouring out without refilling, your glass might be leaky. You're showing up, but not truly receiving. The celebration doesn't land – and neither do you.

Feeling grounded, present and open-hearted? Your glass is full and flowing. You can hold the goodness. You let joy in, you savour the moment and those you share it with.

I offer these reflections gently – as invitations to notice where you are without judgement, with softness and self-compassion. And remember: your glass isn't fixed or broken. You can expand, strengthen and repair it.

When you embrace the shifts of Celebration 2.0 and choose alignment and presence, you expand your capacity to hold celebration – to create joy, to reclaim your fizz. #FizzByDesign

How do you start? As a Celebration Alchemist, your motto is simple: carpe diem. Seize the day, because you know there is no time like the present; you work with what you have, from where you are.

This is the essence of the Celebration Alchemist's Way – an invitation to move through life differently. What follows is a brief overview. You'll find the five intentional steps that bring it to life in Chapter 7.

The Celebration Alchemist Way™

To live as a Celebration Alchemist is to be awake and intentional, to live with more heart, more *you*. It is a different way of seeing, sensing and influencing the world around you. A way that's grounded in the practical magic of turning the ordinary into the extraordinary.

It means:

❖ Living with presence, even when life feels messy

❖ Choosing appreciation, even when joy feels distant

❖ Finding meaning in the everyday, even when no one's watching

It's a way of being for those who:

* ❖ Embody joy, appreciation and celebration as forces for good

* ❖ Choose to live the Life Mixology 2.0 experience – intentional, soulful and joy-led

* ❖ Commit to role-modelling the Pleasure, Power, Purpose and Possibilities of Celebration 2.0

* ❖ Honour the magic in the ordinary and bring the extraordinary to life

And to support this way of living, here is a simple life recipe. It came from Celly, so you know there is a little magic mixed in. She gifted it to me like one of my grandmother's hand-stitched samplers: something to treasure, to live by and to pass on.

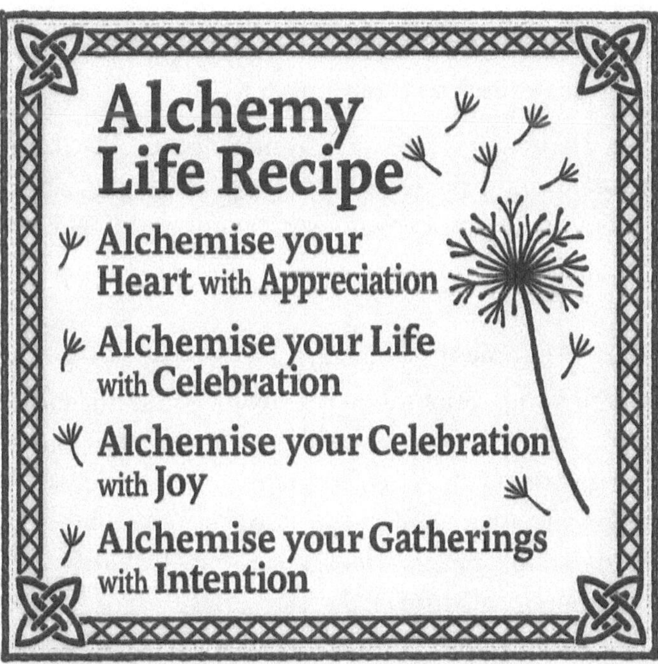

The Celebration Alchemist's Way Celly's recipe and invitation to live with more joy, love and everyday magic.

From Inner Mix to Living Expression

You've met our Spirit of Celebration. You've explored the five Core Elements that bring celebration to life. Maybe you're already sensing some shifts in how you think and feel about celebration.

Now, it's time to move from knowing to doing because Celebration Alchemy lives in practice, not theory. It invites us to translate inner awareness into outer action – to make celebration something we live rather than something we plan.

To help with that, I use three dimensions – three ways of relating to appreciation and celebration that turn awareness into both a daily habit and a shared vibration.

The Three Dimensions of Celebration Alchemy

❖ **Embrace** (Inner Alignment)

❖ **Express** (Everyday Infusions)

❖ **Engage** (Conscious Contribution)

Together, they transform celebration from concept to lived experience – the shift from knowing it matters to actually practising it. Each dimension offers prompts to help you explore, experiment and integrate along the way.

Embrace: Inner Alignment

It all starts with you – your Inner Mix; your bottle filled with all your unique components. You begin by reconnecting with your true energy and values, aligning with SOUL FLOW. You stop waiting for life to feel perfect and start honouring what's real in the moment. You embrace celebration as both a mindset and a practice, recognising it as something that sustains you. From that place of alignment, decisions flow with ease.

> **Example:** The wedding was only weeks away, but tensions were running high. Decisions turned into disagreements. Small details became overwhelming. It wasn't really about the flowers or the table plans; it was the pressure, the exhaustion, the fear of getting it wrong. One evening, as everything came to a head, they stopped.

They sat together. And instead of rehashing the to-do list, they asked themselves: Why are we doing this?

They remembered. It wasn't about orchestrating an impressively perfect day. It was about their love. Their commitment. The beginning of their shared life.

They set a new intention: let every decision flow from love, not fear or expectations. As they reconnected with the truth of their hearts, the pressure eased, the noise quieted. They found their way back to joy and the Spirit of Celebration.

Reflection Prompts for Embrace (Five Core Elements)

→ **Energy:** Where am I pouring energy that doesn't nourish me? Where could I reclaim some?

→ **Intention:** What intention could I set today that aligns with my true values?

→ **Alignment:** Where does my outer life feel out of sync with my inner truth?

→ **Joy:** What's one small thing I can appreciate about myself, right here and now?

→ **Presence:** Did I notice beauty or goodness in one real moment today?

Express: Everyday Infusions

Once grounded in Embrace, appreciation and celebration flow more naturally into everyday life. You start noticing beauty, creating joy in the smallest acts: lighting a candle, offering a compliment, pausing to feel the moment. These are *Everyday Infusions:* small, intentional acts that flavour ordinary life with meaning.

Example: It's late and you're pushing through another round of emails. You notice your jaw is tight, your breath shallow. Instead of ignoring it, you stand, stretch, and open the window. The cool air hits your skin; you take three slow breaths. You put on a song that always makes you smile. For a few minutes, the room feels lighter – and so do you. You haven't escaped the to-do list; you've simply changed the energy.

Reflection Prompts for Express

→ **Energy:** What energy am I bringing into my space today? Do I need to reset it?

→ **Intention:** What ordinary action today could I turn into a small ritual of meaning?

→ **Alignment:** Am I moving through my day from autopilot or awareness?

→ **Joy:** What's one feeling of joy I can create or celebrate right now?

→ **Presence:** How can I pause and re-centre when I feel myself slipping into overdrive?

Engage: Conscious Contribution

Here, celebration becomes relational. You're not waiting for someone else to create the magic; you bring it with you. You sense what others need and offer your energy intentionally. When you bring presence and good energy, it changes the atmosphere. Your joy becomes something others can feel.

Example: At a friend's birthday gathering, even though you have a list of calls to make and emails to catch up on, you intentionally silence your phone and put it away. You set aside the stress, tension and distraction. You choose to be fully present for your friend. You listen deeply. You lift the energy simply by being real and consciously present. You help create the magic without forcing it. And you know what? You might just find it was one of the best nights you've had in a long time.

Reflection Prompts for Engage

> → **Energy:** Where can I offer my energy generously, without depletion or performing for approval?

> → **Intention:** What quiet intention could I hold as I arrive at a shared space today?

> → **Alignment:** Am I showing up as my real self, or the version I think others expect?

> → **Joy:** How might I invite or reflect some joy for someone else today?

> → **Presence:** How can I stay connected and open while engaging with others, even amid distraction?

You've explored the full flow of celebration – how it begins within, ripples through daily life and comes alive in connection with others. Now we step into the spaces where those energies meet: the gatherings where magic multiplies.

Chapter 6
Co-Celebration – Realising the Wonder of Us and the Magic of We

She's standing in the kitchen, wrestling with the zip on her daughter's dress. The babysitter's late. The snacks aren't made. Her husband, already dressed, waits impatiently by the door. She hasn't eaten. She can't find the shoes that go with her dress. They're already late for her friend's wedding.

The journey is fraught with a tight, heavy silence. By the time they arrive, her jaw is clenched, her shoulders are tight and she's holding back tears for reasons she can't even explain. It's a celebration, but she feels barely held together. Exhausted. Emotional. Furious.

This is what showing up often looks like. We arrive at weddings, birthdays, parties and work events under a pile of pressure, distraction and invisible emotional labour. We put on our celebration persona – smile, cheer, toast – yet inside, we're still unravelling from the day, the week, life.

This is not a failure of love or friendship. It's simply the truth: we often land at a celebration without the capacity to actually celebrate. We may be present in body, but absent in spirit.

What if celebration could be something different?

What if it weren't just about turning up, smiling and getting through, but about arriving with presence, energy and intention – and creating something together?

That's the invitation at the heart of the next evolution of celebration: **Co-Celebration.**

The Power of "Co"

In the new paradigm of Celebration 2.0, the "Co" isn't a slogan – it's the shift itself. Because true celebration isn't duty or performance; it's a shared act of creation. We don't just attend an event, we help make it – co-generating energy, co-holding space, co-creating joy. "Co" means we don't orbit around the celebration; we become part of its heartbeat.

Co-Celebration asks us to bring our full selves – not the polished, public ones, but our authentic, present selves. To be aware of how our energy impacts others, and how shared presence can transform a room. To offer generosity of spirit and step beyond ourselves.

When we do, something alchemical happens: celebration stops being something we consume and becomes something consciously communal – a living exchange of joy, meaning and connection.

Real Life – The Reimagined Scene

Remember that scene earlier? The flustered mum, impatient partner, the chaos of simply trying to get out the door. We've all been there.

Let's reimagine it through the lens of Life Mixology and Celebration 2.0. What happens when she checks in with herself in this new way of celebrating?

She pauses in the hallway. It's still messy. She's still flustered and running late. The kids are wild, and hubby now has the car running.

But she stops. She takes a breath. She feels into what she's actually bringing into the day. That's her *Energy*.

She remembers what this is about: her friend is getting married. This is a day of love. She takes a moment to reset and refocus on that. That's her *Intention*.

She's aware of her pattern: frantic last-minute racing, masking the old urge to manage it all, hold it all, be all things to everyone. In that breath, that intention-setting moment, she realises she doesn't have to do it like that anymore. No one truly expects or asks that of her. Only she does. That's her *Alignment*.

She takes another, deeper breath. She chooses to be here, right now. Not racing ahead in her mind. Not fretting. Not predicting. Just *be*. Here. Now. She smiles to herself. That's her *Presence*.

The journey feels different. She and her husband start to get excited; it's their first "date" in so long. They arrive. The bride is late. They take a breath and, hand in hand, they walk to their seats. She smiles, inside and out, as a little shimmer of something delicious stirs within her. Maybe her shoes don't match her dress, but her heart is open. And that shimmer? That's *Joytality*.

That's what celebration looks and feels like in the new paradigm. It's real life, far from perfect, but full of heart, love and joy.

⟋ 5Alive™: Your Inner Celebration Compass

What we just experienced in that wedding scenario is what I call the 5Alive check-in. Think of it as a vibe-check, a way to reorient and realign when something feels off. It's Celebration's Five Core Elements reordered into a simple acronym for easy recall:

A – Aligned: Is how I'm showing up aligned with what I value?

L – Live (Presence): Am I actually here or just "putting in an appearance"?

I – Intentional: What is this celebration about, at heart? What am I choosing?

V – Vital (Joy): Where is the joy in this moment? What would help me reconnect?

E – Energy: What energy am I bringing right now? Am I adding or detracting?

You don't need to check all five every time; just notice what's stirring. Because when even just one element is fully felt and activated, it can shift everything.

Fog or Flow? What Happens When We Don't Check In

We've just seen how a pause can change everything, if we choose to allow it. That simple moment of awareness was a glimpse of Life Mixology 2.0 in action: a celebration lived from presence, not pressure.

The Fog: Celebration 1.0 Default

We've all experienced our own version of that first scenario. It's easy to stay stuck in the same old, ingrained habits. What's harder is stopping, taking responsibility and kicking EGO out of the driver's seat.

And no, the "remixed" scene is not how it usually goes – not yet.

So, before we go further, let's take an honest look at how we often arrive at celebrations unaware of our inner mix or the energy we're carrying. You'll likely recognise some of this:

> → Arriving on autopilot – showing up out of duty or habit, instead of genuine connection.

> → Focusing on what's missing – overthinking, comparing, judging, instead of appreciating what's here.

> → Reacting to invisible expectations – caught in "shoulds," feeling resentment or disappointment, instead of choosing freedom and ease.

> → Worrying about perception – how we're being seen, instead of how we're actually present.

> → Distracted – letting stress, old patterns, or surface-level things like phones hijack us, instead of giving our attention to the moment.

> → If organising – tangled in logistics and worries, instead of actually experiencing the moment you created.

This old way, the Celebration 1.0 default – rushed, distracted, under pressure – stands in sharp contrast to how it can be. It's the familiar EGO mode, whether in overdrive (RAVE) or shutdown (FUNK). And in it, we miss opportunities for connection that are right within reach, if only we could pause and see them. That's not because we don't care; it's because we're human.

The good news is that now you understand more about your inner world; you can start to notice how your mix shows up in life and in celebration. And when you see it, you can shift it.

The Flow: Celebration 2.0 in Action

The magic of alchemy becomes available when we're operating from SOUL FLOW and embodying **5Alive:** Aligned, Live (Presence), Intentional, Vital (Joy) and Energy.

Let's take a real example.

There's a woman, let's call her "Sally." She came across this book (quiet plug here) and something about it caught her attention. She began reading it in quiet moments, trying out the 5Alive check-ins at home. She started noticing how her improved energy affected her mood, her kids, the flow of her day. Nothing radical, just some small, subtle shifts. The tension in the mornings eased. Her son smiled more. Even dinner felt lighter.

One Sunday night, when the usual "Monday morning-itis" kicked in with the 9 p.m. news bulletin, she reached for 5Alive again. This time, a thought dropped in: *Could this work at the office, too?*

So she tried it. A check-in before a Monday meeting. A breath before delivering feedback. At first, it felt clunky, even a little forced. Midweek, she almost gave up. Then Friday arrived.

Her team had wrapped a huge project. Normally, she'd call a stand-up to review and move on. Everyone was tired, ready to bolt. But this time, Sally paused.

> → **A – Aligned:** She remembered what she really wanted for herself and the team – more connection, less stress, genuine camaraderie.

> → **L – Live (Presence):** She took a breath, grounded herself and arrived fully in the moment.

> → **I – Intentional:** She refocused on her deeper intention: not just to tick a box, but to help each person feel seen and appreciated.

> → **V – Vital (Joy):** She noticed her energy – steady, open, generous – and chose to let that warmth lead.

> → **E – Energy:** She grounded that feeling, carrying it with her as she stepped forward.

Then she said simply, "I've decided the review can wait until Monday. Instead, I just want to celebrate what we did – and how we did it."

She named names. Called out effort and kindness. Others joined in. Someone shared a story. One guy, usually silent, spoke up. His voice cracked with emotion. The team applauded as one. Someone pulled out treats. Music played quietly from a phone. People lingered. It wasn't grand or planned. But it was real.

This is Co-Celebration in action. When appreciation and celebration become a way of showing up – not reserved for special occasions – we start co-creating joy in the simple, ordinary moments that usually slip by.

That's the real magic of Celebration Alchemy.

The Hidden Power of Co-Celebration *(A sprinkle of research if you're the curious type)*

We've seen Co-Celebration is about presence, meaning and shared humanity. It has profound beneficial effects on us, individually and collectively. When we celebrate together, something remarkable happens: joy multiplies. As we touched on earlier, this isn't just feel-good theory – it's backed by science. Here's a snapshot of the key findings:

Science Snapshot

1. **Joy Spreads**

   Emotional Contagion Effect

   Mirror Neurons

2. **Joy Deepens When Shared**

   Synergy Effect

   Celebration Multiplier Effect

   Science of Capitalisation

3. **Joy Transforms Us**

   Broaden-and-Build Theory

   Michelangelo Effect

   Ritual Effect

The Science Behind The Magic

❖ *The Emotional Contagion Effect: Joy Is Infectious*

Think of emotions like glitter: once one person brings it, it gets *everywhere.* Neuroscience shows that when we radiate joy, excitement or appreciation, those around us automatically absorb and reflect that energy. That's why one person's joy can lift an entire room.[1]

❖ *Mirror Neurons: The Brain's Magic Mirror*

Ever noticed how a giggle fit spreads through a group like wildfire? That's mirror neurons in action. Our brains are wired to copy the emotions and actions of those around us. So when you're fully present, engaged and celebrating authentically, you invite others into the same joy without even trying.[2]

---

1   Elaine Hatfield, John T. Cacioppo, and Richard L. Rapson, *Emotional Contagion* (Cambridge, England: Cambridge University Press, 1993).

2   Marco Iacoboni, *Mirroring People: The New Science of Empathy and How We Connect with Others* (New York: Farrar, Straus and Giroux, 2008).

❖ *The Synergy Effect: Shared Experiences Are More Meaningful*

Even simple moments, like watching a film, feel more enjoyable when shared. One study found chocolate tasted better when eaten at the same time as another person, even without interaction; the simple act of sharing heightened enjoyment.[3] Celebration works the same way: the shared experience deepens the pleasure.

❖ *The Celebration Multiplier Effect: Why Joy Grows When Shared*

Most things diminish when shared, but not joy. The more we co-celebrate, the more we scale happiness, deepen bonds and strengthen communities. Studies show that leaders who foster a culture of appreciation and celebration create stronger teams, happier relationships and more engaged communities.[4] That's why intentional appreciation – at home, at work, in gatherings – creates ripples far beyond a single moment

❖ *The Science of Capitalisation: Why Sharing Good News Matters*

Sharing good news boosts happiness even more than the event itself. Studies show that when we talk about and relive positive experiences with others and they respond enthusiastically, the emotional benefits expand, turning small wins into powerful moments of connection and joy.[5] This brings home the value of taking time to share and celebrate even everyday achievements.

❖ *The Broaden-and-Build Theory of Positive Emotions: Joy Expands Possibilities*

Positive emotions don't just feel good; they make us better humans. Research shows that joy helps us think more creatively, build stronger relationships and create longer-lasting memories. When we celebrate together, we literally rewire our brains for more connection and resilience.[6]

---

3   Erica J. Boothby, Margaret S. Clark, and John A. Bargh, "Shared Experiences Are Amplified," *Psychological Science* 25, no. 12 (December 2014): 2209–16, doi:10.1177/0956797614551162.

4   Ed Diener and Martin E. P. Seligman, "Very Happy People," *Psychological Science* 13, no. 1 (January 2002): 81–84, doi:10.1111/1467-9280.00415.

5   Shelly L. Gable, Harry T. Reis, Emily A. Impett, and Evan R. Asher, "What Do You Do When Things Go Right? The Intrapersonal and Interpersonal Benefits of Sharing Positive Events," *Journal of Personality and Social Psychology* 87, no. 2 (August 2004): 228–45, doi:10.1037/0022-3514.87.2.228.

❖ *The Michelangelo Effect: Sculpting Each Other's Best Selves*

Just like Michelangelo chipped away at marble to reveal the masterpiece within, our celebrations "sculpt" each other. When we celebrate someone, we reinforce their best qualities, helping them own their full potential. Simply put, your appreciation can help enhance someone's confidence, growth and self-belief.[7]

❖ *The Ritual Effect: Why Humans Have Always Celebrated Together*

From ancient feasts to modern weddings, humans have always used shared rituals to create social glue. The strongest communities – whether families, friendships or workplaces – are the ones that celebrate intentionally. When we neglect communal joy, we risk loneliness, disengagement and weaker relationships.[8]

Co-Celebration is our Social Superpower: it rewires us, bonds us and sustains us.

6 Barbara L. Fredrickson, "The Role of Positive Emotions in Positive Psychology: The Broaden-and-Build Theory of Positive Emotions," *American Psychologist* 56, no. 3 (March 2001): 218–26, doi:10.1037//0003-066X.56.3.218.

7 Stephen M. Drigotas, Caryl E. Rusbult, and Jennifer Wieselquist, "Close Partner as Sculptor of the Ideal Self: Behavioral Affirmation and the Michelangelo Phenomenon," *Journal of Personality and Social Psychology* 77, no. 2 (September 1999): 293–323, doi:10.1037/0022-3514.77.2.293.

8 James H. Fowler and Nicholas A. Christakis, "Dynamic Spread of Happiness in a Large Social Network: Longitudinal Analysis Over 20 Years in the Framingham Heart Study," *British Medical Journal* 337 (2008): a2338.

Honouring the Full Spectrum of Co-Celebration

We've seen how Co-Celebration transforms our joyful moments – multiplying joy, deepening connection, rewiring us for resilience. But this power isn't limited to celebrations of success or happy milestones. It extends to every moment that connects us, every experience that bonds us, every transition we walk through together.

Co-Celebration is as much about showing up in sorrow as it is in joy. We don't just acknowledge life's peaks, we support each other in its valleys too.

Some of the most sacred Co-Celebration happens in quiet, tender spaces: funerals, memorials, celebrations of life, moments of collective grief. These, too, are acts of shared presence. They are powerful expressions of love, memory and the legacy someone leaves behind. They remind us that celebration doesn't exclude sorrow; it holds it and helps carry those who are grieving.

And when we gather in those moments with intention, grace and connection, we experience a different kind of joy: a gentle, reverent joy. The kind that honours life, even as we say goodbye.

These sacred moments are Co-Celebration in its most heartfelt, human form. They offer us a chance to connect deeply to what's sacred, to embody compassion and to express love through presence and support. They reflect what community truly means. We can sense the presence of the Spirit of Celebration strongly in these moments. She's always with us, in the laughter, the toasts, the music. But here, in the stillness of loss and sorrow, her presence wraps around us. She brings breath, solace and space to feel and heal. She helps us hold what's too big to carry alone.

Is Your Celebration Nourishing or Just Filling?

Whether in joy or in sorrow, we've seen that Co-Celebration holds profound power. But not all gatherings actually nourish us. Some leave us feeling drained, disconnected or simply off.

The reality is that celebration, in any form, can either sustain us or deplete us. Some moments leave us heavy, overstimulated or strangely empty – the social version of an overindulgent "all-you-can-eat-buffet." Noisy and overwhelming, it never quite satisfies – whether you've piled your plate too high or sat back picking at the edges. And often the unease lingers afterwards, in that familiar post-party replay of what we said, did or didn't do, instead of feeling genuinely uplifted.

Now contrast that with something beautifully simple: a shared meal, prepared together with care. The joy of choosing good ingredients. Laughter around the table, with space to breathe and savour.

The deeper truth here is that it isn't really about what's on the table; it's about how we choose to partake. We can fall into old, habitual ways of coping, stuffing down feelings and trying to fill the void. Or we can bring discernment and intention, choosing the kind of celebration that leaves us lighter, more connected, with an aftertaste that nourishes instead of nags.

Celebration 2.0 is not about consuming more, but about nourishing better, quality over quantity, presence over performance. It's celebration as soul food.

Ask yourself: *Is my celebrating weighing me down ... or lightening me?*

Your Energy Matters: The Alchemy of Contribution

We don't just attend celebrations; we actively contribute to the vibe. We're either unconsciously draining the energy or consciously lifting it. You've seen that every celebration is a co-creation. Celebration Alchemists live with the awareness of this power and responsibility. Whether as hosts or attendees, we influence the atmosphere. In Celebration 2.0, we each take ownership of the energy we bring, the presence we offer and the atmosphere we help set. We do this by choosing to show up in SOUL FLOW, embodying and sharing joy generously. I call this being a "Joy Catalyst."

The Joy Catalyst™: Embodying Co-Celebration

#FizzByDesign – joy that spreads through energy, not effort,
like seeds carried on the breeze.

Something shifts when you're fully present and genuinely connected to both the moment and the people around you. You stop thinking about how you should celebrate and simply allow yourself to be fully alive to what's unfolding.

You don't need to run the show or step into the spotlight; presence doesn't have to be loud to be felt. Sometimes it's a quiet calm that helps others settle. Other times it's a playful spark that lifts the energy. Either way, when you show up as a Joy Catalyst, people around you feel more at ease, more open, more themselves.

Joy Catalysts create joy that spreads naturally – contagious through energy, not effort.

Every one of us has this potential. The choice is whether we default to Celebration 1.0 habits (wondering if it'll be fun, what we'll get out of it) or intentionally show up to co-create something great. When we engage fully, appreciate what's been created and add joy to the mix, we transform the atmosphere.

Celebration isn't just the host's or organiser's responsibility – it's the collective's. This is the essence of Co-Celebration.

Mixing the Right Energy: Your Inner and Outer Celebration Expressions

Let's explore this through Life Mixology. We've seen how your **Signature Mix** – your inner baseline – flows into your **Celebration Cocktail,** the way your energy shifts when you're preparing to celebrate. But something else happens when you stop thinking about celebrating and actually step into it. Your Inner Mix reblends into your **Co-Celebration Style™,** the way others experience you.

Understanding how these connect gives you real power over your presence. Let me show you how this works in real life.

From Alone to Together: How Your Mix Evolves

Picture this: you're home alone, doing your thing. Whatever the activity, there's a mood behind it – calm, anxious, joyful, flat. That's your **Signature Mix.** Just you, with you. Your inner baseline.

Later, you're getting ready for a party. Your nervous system starts gearing up. Your social brain begins scanning: *Who'll be there? Will I fit in? What happened last time?* Let's be honest, your brain doesn't remember the ninety-nine great outings; it seizes on the one time you felt left out or invisible (think back to SCARF triggers).

In EGO mode, you start adding ingredients without realising: perfectionism, self-doubt, overthinking. You mute your true voice before you've even left the house. In SOUL FLOW, you mix with care: calm, curiosity, openness. Even if that awkward moment pops up, you see it with perspective.

That shift – your baseline stirred by social preparation – is your **Celebration Cocktail** forming.

Then you arrive and engage. How you interact – whether you hug or hover, cheerlead or fade out – becomes your **Co-Celebration Style:** the visible expression of everything you've been mixing inside.

Your Co-Celebration Style *- You bringing your Inner Mix into shared moments – how you engage with others.*

Think of your Celebration Cocktail as a perfume (or aftershave) you wear; when you walk into a room, people catch the scent instantly. Your Co-Celebration Style is how you move in that room – your social choreography.

Why Understanding These Layers Helps

When you understand these layers, you can sense when stress is warping your vibe and course-correct before it pours out. You stop assuming intention equals impact.

In EGO mode, we might *intend* to be fun or easy-going, but if we're also trying to control how we're seen, our energy gets murky. Others feel that tension, even when we don't mean it. That's the difference between what we think we're bringing and what others actually feel from us.

Most of us have been conditioned to scan for approval or adjust ourselves to avoid rejection. When we're sensitive, it's easy to get caught up in stories about how we're being received. But here's an important reminder: we can't – and shouldn't try to – control how others perceive us. How people respond isn't always a reflection of our energy. Sometimes, they're caught in their own storm – hurting, defensive, tired, or just dealing with something we can't see. We don't always know what someone's carrying, so be kind, practice empathy and don't take things too personally.

Surrendering the need to manage everything creates space for something deeper. When you honour what's true for you – without judging or worrying – you show up in SOUL FLOW: anchored in your values, available and generous. You are not scanning the room wondering, *Am I too much?* or *Did I get that right?* You already know your heart is true. That soul-level intention is what people feel most. That's what it means to lead with energy – the shift from control to connection. This is the art of Co-Celebration in action.

So how do you begin to recognise your own patterns and the impact your energy has on others?

Let's pause and check in right now:

> → How do you tend to show up at celebrations – rushed, excited, hesitant, hyped?
>
> → What throws your mix off?
>
> → How might that energy spill over to others?
>
> → Is there anything you'd like to mix differently?

You can use this check-in anytime – before a gathering, during it, or afterwards as a reflection.

Discovering Your Mix with the Enneagram

You've seen how much our patterns – formed by our inner narrative – affect our energy. And as mixologists, we know that understanding the ingredients and how to work with them is the path to master craftsmanship. The Enneagram, which we touched on earlier, is a powerful tool for this kind of unpacking. It reveals nine core personality energies, each with distinct habits, motivations and stress triggers. It helps you see how your inner world colours your outer impact.

In this next section, you'll meet the nine Enneagram energies we'll be exploring. These are:

1. **The Perfectionist**

2. **The Giver**

3. **The Achiever**

4. The Individualist

5. The Observer

6. The Loyalist

7. The Enthusiast

8. The Challenger

9. The Peacemaker

Each type has both an EGO expression (stressed/reactive) and a SOUL FLOW expression (aligned/grounded). The Enneagram helps you notice your default and growth patterns, especially in relationships and group dynamics. It's a lens for seeing where your energy goes under pressure and in connection with others – and how you come alive when you're aligned with essence.

For each type, we'll explore how the Signature Mix, Celebration Cocktail, and Co-Celebration Style show up in both EGO and SOUL states.

Understanding what we bring – and how it affects others and the overall vibe – helps us choose our *desired* impact instead of defaulting to autopilot.

Here's a visual contrast of default versus intentional party mixes – two very different vibes depending on what each of us is *energetically pouring*.

When EGO stirs the mix, glasses clash and moods collide, throwing the collective feel:

Co-Celebration Party Mix: EGO Tray *– our mix under stress. When EGO leads, the pour goes off-balance: flavours clash, tensions rise and energy dips.*

When we're in SOUL FLOW, everyone's tuned in, aware of their own rhythm, and the whole vibe sparkles joyfully:

Co-Celebration Party Mix: SOUL Tray – our mix when aligned. In SOUL FLOW, flavours balance, joy fizzes and the room hums.

You've just seen how our individual energy mix shifts the vibe – from tension to harmony, from effort to ease.

Now let's explore these mixes in more detail. Even if you don't know your type, you'll recognise familiar patterns. This is a light-touch guide – take what helps you make sense of your celebration presence, no need to over-think it. Whether you're more burnt espresso martini or fizzy rosé, this is #MixNotFix.

Once you understand your ingredients, you can shift from automatic pouring to intentional mixing – showing up with presence, energy and intention. As you read, don't look for perfection; look for resonance. If something sparks a strong reaction, note it; resistance often points to recognition.

Type 1: The Perfectionist

Do you find yourself mentally rewriting the playlist, or spotting everything that's not quite right?

EGO Expression

❖ **Signature Mix:** Inner Perfectionism – *self-critical, high internal standards*

❖ **Celebration Cocktail:** Control Freak Cosmo – *everything measured, not much felt*

❖ **Co-Celebration Style:** Celebration Critic – *rigid, restrained, holding back joy until it's "done properly"*

When stressed, you scan for flaws instead of feeling joy, and the urge to get things right overrides the invitation to simply enjoy.

SOUL Expression

❖ **Signature Mix:** Purposeful Precision – *clarity without the clenching*

❖ **Celebration Cocktail:** Let-It-Go Limoncello Spritz – *bright, light, ready to relax*

❖ **Co-Celebration Style:** Detail Hero – *brings calm presence, not silent pressure*

When aligned, your discernment becomes a gift. You model that excellence doesn't need tension.

The shift: From energy editor to celebration enhancer, from tightening control to trusting joy.

Grounding reminder: *There's nothing to prove when you're present. Let joy be imperfect.*

Type 2: The Giver

Are you topping up glasses, checking in, holding the emotional reins of the room?

EGO Expression

❖ **Signature Mix:** Over-Attuned – *turned down to self, tuned into everyone else*

❖ **Celebration Cocktail:** People-Pleaser Punch – *sweet, over-poured, secretly exhausting*

❖ **Co-Celebration Style:** Over-Attender – *giving, giving, giving … then disappearing*

Your care turns into over-functioning. You tend to everyone else's joy while neglecting your own, forgetting that your presence is enough.

SOUL Expression

❖ **Signature Mix:** Heartfelt Generosity – *open, grounded, self-honouring*

❖ **Celebration Cocktail:** Overflowing Love Bellini – *joyful, self-love, engaged*

❖ **Co-Celebration Style:** Glow Guide – *generous, warm, inclusive*

When anchored in your worth, your warmth becomes radiant. You give with ease and receive with grace.

The shift: From over-giving to open-hearted receiving. From self-sacrificing to joyful participant.

Grounding reminder: *You don't have to pour from empty. The moment is fuller when you are, too.*

Type 3: The Achiever

Do you catch yourself performing, scanning for feedback, turning celebration into something to win?

EGO Expression

- ❖ **Signature Mix:** Image-Fuelled Drive – *always on, always proving*
- ❖ **Celebration Cocktail:** Trophy Espresso Martini – *bold, polished, performative*
- ❖ **Co-Celebration Style:** Spotlight Seeker – *in it to win it, even when there's no competition*

Celebration becomes a stage. You show up polished but not present, focused more on how it looks rather than feels.

SOUL Expression

- ❖ **Signature Mix:** Authentic Radiance – *driven by meaning, not metrics*
- ❖ **Celebration Cocktail:** True Joy Gimlet – *crisp, refreshing, authentic*
- ❖ **Co-Celebration Style:** Wow Spotlighter – *celebrates what's real, not impressive*

Your confidence becomes natural and energising. You connect without curating, lead without over-delivering.

The shift: From performing success to living joy. From standout actor to soul-connected celebrator.

Grounding reminder: *You don't need to impress joy. It already knows who you are.*

Type 4: The Individualist

Do you feel like no one else is quite feeling the moment like you are? Something's missing?

EGO Expression

- ❖ **Signature Mix:** Emotional Intensity – *yearning for something more*
- ❖ **Celebration Cocktail:** Melancholy Merlot – *brooding elegance, deep, complex, removed*
- ❖ **Co-Celebration Style:** Air Kisser – *present, but not quite connected*

Celebration feels shallow or disappointing. You crave depth, but that longing leaves you lingering on the edge.

SOUL Expression

- ❖ **Signature Mix:** Soulful Clarity – *centred, rich, beautifully open*
- ❖ **Celebration Cocktail:** Vibrant Sangria – *layered, vibrant, full of life*
- ❖ **Co-Celebration Style:** Depth Whisperer – *connects deeply, delights freely*

Your emotional awareness becomes a gift. You find meaning in the moment, without needing it to be more.

The shift: From romantic outsider to participant. From watching the moment to being in it.

Grounding reminder: *Not everything has to feel profound to be worth feeling.*

Type 5: The Observer

Do you hang back, take it all in and keep a little distance – even when you're glad to be there?

EGO Expression

- ❖ **Signature Mix:** Withheld Presence – *analysis paralysis*

- ❖ **Celebration Cocktail:** Energy-Saver Negroni – *conserving energy while mentally preparing*

- ❖ **Co-Celebration Style:** Silent Witness – *quietly observing, rarely engaging*

You keep energy close, analysing dynamics rather than joining in. Safer, but less connected.

SOUL Expression

- ❖ **Signature Mix:** Calm Enquirer– *perceptive, curious*

- ❖ **Celebration Cocktail:** Curious Clover Club – *smooth, confident, interested*

- ❖ **Co-Celebration Style:** Quiz Master – *thoughtful, witty, engaging*

Thoughtful presence, quiet humour, not needing to be the life of the party, but belongs in it.

The shift: From quiet observer to steady contributor. From buffered to meaningful presence.

Grounding reminder: *What you say lands, and your wisdom makes you part of the moment.*

Type 6: The Loyalist

Do you check the exits, guest list and worst-case scenarios before letting go?

EGO Expression

❖ **Signature Mix:** Vigilance Spiral – *spinning through self-doubt, always on*

❖ **Celebration Cocktail:** Anxiety on the Rocks – *braced and cautious, always vigilant*

❖ **Co-Celebration Style:** Barcoder – *scanning the room, but never quite relaxing in it*

You struggle to fully trust the moment. Running backup plans while keeping things steady, but never quite relaxing.

SOUL Expression

❖ **Signature Mix:** Grounded Assurance – *steady, trusting and present*

❖ **Celebration Cocktail:** Trust-the-Moment Mojito – *grounded freshness, open, reassured*

❖ **Co-Celebration Style:** Flow Fortifier – *anchors connection without needing control*

You bring quiet strength without needing to anticipate everything, allowing space for surprise.

The shift: From scanning for danger to showing up with faith. From cautious protector to calm anchor.

Grounding reminder: *You don't have to plan for everything to be safe.*

Type 7: The Enthusiast

Do you bounce from moment to moment, seeking the next thrill or escape route?

EGO Expression

- ❖ **Signature Mix:** Scattered Stimulation – *chasing highs, dodging depth*

- ❖ **Celebration Cocktail:** FOMO Fireball Daiquiri – *bold, sugary, gone too soon*

- ❖ **Co-Celebration Style:** Social Butterfly – *fluttering everywhere, landing nowhere*

The moment never feels like enough. You keep things bright, but miss what you came for.

SOUL Expression

- ❖ **Signature Mix:** Joyful Calm – *playful, fully alive, at ease*

- ❖ **Celebration Cocktail:** Fully Present Passionfruit Martini – *bold, bright, deeply satisfying*

- ❖ **Co-Celebration Style:** Vibe Magician – *turns presence into pleasure, lights the room*

Your joy becomes centred. You savour what's here, bring others into the moment. You integrate meaning and fun.

The shift: From chasing highs to inhabiting joy. From scattered light to intentional shine.

Grounding reminder: *You don't have to go everywhere to feel everything.*

Type 8: The Challenger

Do you walk in ready to lead, protect, or power through, just in case?

EGO Expression

❖ **Signature Mix:** Intense Core – *raw power hijacks feelings*

❖ **Celebration Cocktail:** Power Play Whiskey Sour – *ready to control, connection turned down*

❖ **Co-Celebration Style:** Demander – *potent, sets tone, can shut others down*

Celebration becomes something to manage. Big energy, bold leadership, but sometimes leaves no room for softer voices.

SOUL Expression

❖ **Signature Mix:** Open Strength – *grounded, generous, emotionally available*

❖ **Celebration Cocktail:** Full-hearted Old Fashioned – *strong, smooth, balanced*

❖ **Co-Celebration Style:** Inclusive Ally – *creates space for others to shine*

Strength becomes steady. You lead by example, allow others in, show that power includes vulnerability.

The shift: From force to flow. From dominating the room to deepening the connection.

Grounding reminder: *You don't lose power by softening.*

Type 9: The Peacemaker

Do you go with the flow, hold back preferences, or keep things smooth at your expense?

EGO Expression

- ❖ **Signature Mix:** Comfortable Disconnection – *feels fine but softly checked out*

- ❖ **Celebration Cocktail:** Go-With-the-Flow Fizz – *light, easy, a little too mellow*

- ❖ **Co-Celebration Style:** Peace Zoner – *present in body, vague in energy*

You keep things undemanding by silencing your opinions and downplaying your desires to keep the peace.

SOUL Expression

- ❖ **Signature Mix:** Embodied Harmony – *calm, connected and centred*

- ❖ **Celebration Cocktail:** Happy Highball – *refreshing, real, quietly radiant*

- ❖ **Co-Celebration Style:** Ease Connector – *brings lightness with presence and voice*

You speak up when it matters, contributing to the vibe. True harmony includes your voice.

The shift: From quiet blending to conscious belonging. From fading out to showing up.

Grounding reminder: *You don't have to keep the peace by losing your presence.*

Why This Matters

You've just sampled nine different flavours of how our inner mix interacts in celebration. This isn't about labelling yourself or getting it "right" – it's about awareness, the foundation for showing up as a Celebration Alchemist. Once you understand your vibe, you can shift it. When you know your Signature Mix and what you bring through your Celebration Cocktail, you can craft an authentic Co-Celebration Style – one that positively influences the energy for everyone.

Your mix isn't a fixed identity. It shifts with mood, mindset, stress and alignment. #MixNotFix; you always have a choice:

→ Am I celebrating from **EGO** or **SOUL**?

→ Am I energising or draining?

→ Am I co-creating or controlling?

When you show up with intention, generosity and presence, you become a Joy Catalyst. And that's the heart of living Celebration Alchemy.

Here's a way to check in, align and show up as a Celebration Alchemist:

Active Engagement Checklist

☐ **Arrive with intention.** Choose to bring warmth, presence and positive energy.

☐ **Be fully present.** Put the phone (or distraction of choice) down. Connect to what's happening now.

☐ **Let go of perfection.** Focus on connection, not control.

☐ **Contribute more than you consume.** Appreciate what's already here. Bring energy, not just expectations.

☐ **Be a celebration enhancer.** Lead with generosity and curiosity, not complaints or critique.

☐ **Own your influence.** Your energy affects the room – it's contagious. Use it consciously.

☐ **Co-create the moment.** Contribute authentically and consciously. You're part of the collective vibe.

☐ **Be a Joy Catalyst.** You don't need the mic or the spotlight, just your presence, offered with heart.

Remember: your presence is the real present. Bring it fully, and you'll never leave a celebration empty.

Chapter 7
Living the Celebration Alchemist Way

Bringing Celebration 2.0 to Life – One Step at a Time

This chapter is your practical reference guide for living the Celebration Alchemist's Way. In Chapter 5 we named the *way* as we began the shift from inner mix to living expression. Here, we put it into practice through five simple, intentional steps.

Key Reminders

→ You don't need to throw everything out; Life Mixology reminds us that we're not broken, just refining our mix. #MixNotFix

→ With awareness comes alignment, and with alignment comes joy.

→ Celly, the Spirit of Celebration, is your quiet pulse of appreciation, a reminder there's always something to notice. #MakingMomentsMatter

Five Intentional Steps of The Celebration Alchemist's Way

Living the Celebration Alchemist's Way means holding two threads at once:

❖ You're alchemising celebration itself, transforming it from pressure and performance into something pleasurable.

❖ You're alchemising your life, using celebration as a lens for more appreciation, connection and joy.

For easy recall, think of these steps as your 5 S's:

1: **Start** with You – Check Your State

2: **Select** Your Ingredients – Choose How You Want to Show Up

3: **Stir** with Intention – Move with Purpose

4: **Savour** the Sip – Embrace the Moment

5: **Share** the Sparkle – Be a Joy Catalyst

These steps are prompts, not rules. They become your celebratory compass. Adapt them to your own pace. Use them anytime: to prepare before an event, when things feel off, or for deeper intention setting.

Step 1: Start with You – Check Your State

Catch the vibe before it catches you.

Before you can celebrate anything, you've got to check in with yourself. Are you tense, tuned out or trying too hard?

> **Example:** You're invited to a friend's birthday bash, but you're just not feeling it. You stare at your outfit options, wondering if you should bail. Instead of ghosting or guilt-tripping yourself, you pause and notice you're in shutdown mode – flat, overthinking, disconnected (FUNK). That self-awareness gives you choice: shift your vibe or stay home with intention, not avoidance.

✐ **EGO Check-In™**

A quick scan for whether EGO is running the show. Ask yourself:

→ What am I feeling right now? (Tight? Heavy? Wired? Numb?)

→ Is this overdrive (RAVE) or shutdown (FUNK)?

→ What do I actually need? (To breathe? To rest? To show up differently?)

Common patterns to notice:

→ Overdrive (RAVE): Rushing, reactive, validation-seeking, staying busy to avoid discomfort, overthinking.

→ Shutdown (FUNK): Fearful, flat, emotionally checked out, keeping small to stay safe.

Remember: EGO isn't the enemy; it's your internal alarm system. Just breathe, notice and choose what's next.

Step 2: Select Your Ingredients – Choose How You Want to Show Up

What energy do I want to flavour this moment with?

You've noticed what's happening. Now choose how you want to show up. This isn't forced positivity; it's clarifying your intention and energy.

Example: You're heading to a family dinner, mind racing, phone buzzing. Before walking in, you pause: what kind of energy do you want to bring?

/ SOUL FLOW Check-In™

A reflective prompt to choose from essence, not old habits.

Choose one SOUL quality to guide you right now:

→ *Self-Aware:* Am I noticing what's truly present for me right now?

→ *Open-Hearted:* Am I approaching this with curiosity or judgement?

→ *Unique:* Am I expressing what's true for me, not what's expected?

→ *Legacy-focused:* Am I thinking beyond this moment to what matters long-term?

When you ground yourself in any of these SOUL qualities, you naturally access FLOW: becoming more Flexible, Light, Optimistic and Willing. This is SOUL FLOW – your full essence in action.

Just one quality is enough to bring you back to yourself.

Step 3: Stir with Intention – Move with Purpose

What does my energy need right now?

You've checked your state and chosen your intention. Now follow through, even in small ways.

> **Example:** At a work event, you set an intention to be open-hearted, but a colleague's passive-aggressive remark throws you off. Instead of reacting, you pause and take a breath. You notice the part of you that wants to react, but you also sense what's really needed: a reset before engaging.

That reset might look different depending on your state. Here are four simple ways to shift your energy.

✎ Energy Reset – Shake, Stir, Blend, Rest

Sense what your system needs when you feel off. These resets can be big or small, physical or subtle – adapt them to your context.

Feel tense or agitated?

> → *Shake:* dance it off, shake it out, then follow with calming breaths.

Feel flat or disconnected?

> → *Stir:* intentionally reawaken with music, fresh air or something delightful.

Feel scattered or overwhelmed?

→ *Blend:* Pause and centre by using your breath or a journal jot.

Feel exhausted or depleted?

→ *Rest:* honour your needs, stop pushing, step back and replenish.

One intentional shift can change the energy, for you and for others.

Step 4: Savour the Sip – Embrace the Moment

Be. Here. Now.

> *"The best and most beautiful things in the world cannot be seen or even touched – they must be felt with the heart."* – Helen Keller

You've checked in, chosen your mix and followed through. Now pause and receive. This is about presence, not in big gestures, but in the small moments that matter.

> **Example:** You're at a dinner party, surrounded by people you care about, but your head's in work mode. Conversations swirl around you, but you're not really in them. Laughter cuts through the mental noise; you manage to catch a joke that cracks the table up. You breathe into the lightness, seeing the faces around you, the people that matter, and you savour the moment.

Here's a simple practice to help you do that more often:

/ **CHEERS**

A simple way to pause and anchor what's good, meaningful and worth remembering.

> **C** – *Choose to pause.* This is your cue to notice, to catch the moment before it slips by.

> **H** – *Honour the moment.* Acknowledge that it matters, that you want to feel it.

> **E** – *Embrace it.* Slow your breath. Quiet your thoughts. Open to what you're feeling.

> **E** – *Engage with it.* Activate your senses: what do you see, hear, taste, smell, feel? Let it sink in.

> **R** – *Reflect on it.* Why does it matter to you?

> **S** – *Savour (and maybe share).* Smile. Linger. Tell someone, or journal it for yourself.

What you feel fully, you can access later. This is what makes joy durable and turns the fleeting into something fulfilling.

Step 5: Share the Sparkle – Be a Joy Catalyst

Joy shared is joy multiplied.

Celebration isn't always confetti. Sometimes, it's the right story shared at just the right time.

> **Example:** You're at a memorial for someone much loved. The room feels heavy, suspended in uncomfortable silence. Something tugs at you – a memory of something ridiculous they once said at a party that became an inside joke. You feel called to share it. Silence, then a chuckle, then a sob-laugh from the widow that releases something. Another memory is offered, then another. The grief's still there, but now there's laughter between tears. A remembering of their light, a glint of shared humanity, of love.

And yes, sometimes it is confetti and dance floors and pure delight.

That's the power of sharing – whether it's releasing grief through laughter at a memorial or lighting up a dance floor. Your presence can shift the energy in a room. This is about those contagious moments – the small but powerful ways you catalyse connection, spark possibility and invite others in. Here's how to practice being a Joy Catalyst:

⁄ SPLASH Effect™

A playful prompt for how to embody Co-Celebration with heart, spark and presence.

> **S**pill joy – *let it pour from your presence; you've got the Licence.*

> **P**ause for pleasure – *notice what delights; choose to savour.*

> **L**augh out loud – *don't mute your joy; let it be heard, felt and shared.*

> **A**ctivate magic – *bring your unique buzz; shift the vibe and open space.*

> **S**hare generously – *offer your attention, stories and smile; freely and fully.*

> **H**ave fun – *joy is contagious and you're the carrier; life's too short not to.*

SPLASH: You as a Joy Catalyst, you in SOUL FLOW.

Bringing It All Together

These five steps are your go-to practice for more joy, presence and authentic celebration – a simple pathway from checking in with yourself to sharing joy with others.

And remember the Three Dimensions of Celebration Alchemy? The five steps are how you live them day to day:

> **Embrace** (Steps 1 and 2) – Inner alignment: checking your state and choosing your intention

> **Express** (Steps 3 and 4) – Everyday Infusions: taking purposeful action and savouring moments

Engage (Step 5) – Conscious contribution: sharing joy with others.

Every time you use the steps or tools, you embody the alchemical journey of living joyfully, making the ordinary extraordinary. And in doing so, you awaken the possibility of joy for others too.

If you're wondering how to start, here's what the research says:

→ **Start small.** Tiny habits lead to lasting change.

→ **Stay consistent.** Regular micro-practices beat big, occasional efforts.

→ **Build gradually.** Layering change over time makes it stick.

As a Celebration Alchemist, you know not to wait for the perfect conditions. Remember *"carpe diem"* – start now where you are, with what you have. Each small act of presence, appreciation or intention strengthens your capacity to celebrate and rewires your brain to see more joy.

This is how real change happens: not in one grand leap, but through small moments that matter.

#MakingMomentsMatter

Here's a simple visual showing how the Celebration Alchemist's Way restores your glass – strengthening your capacity for joy and celebration:

*The Celebration Alchemist Way: Dimensions and Everyday Infusions
for the mindset and practice of Celebration 2.0*

Next, we'll explore what happens when you're not only living celebration for yourself, but creating it for others – when your inner Alchemist becomes the Alchemiser, also known as the Organiser.

SECTION 4
Celebration Alchemistry for Organisers – Where Energy Meets Design

We shift focus now to those who create the spaces and gatherings where celebration takes form: the hosts, planners and organisers.

This section is for all of you – the ones bringing live experiences together with care and effort, often at personal cost and without the recognition you deserve.

The power to transform celebration – to realise its full potential – lies most powerfully in the hands of those who orchestrate it: you.

When you bring Celebration Alchemist energy to organising, you channel personal clarity into design, flow and the experience itself. You create intentionally, with legacy as your compass. This is becoming a **Celebration Alchemiser.**

Here's where we go next: we'll explore nine different Organising Styles, using the Enneagram again as the lens to reveal the patterns that drive us under pressure and the strengths that guide us when we're aligned. We'll also explore an alchemical framework for designing intentional experiences with greater ease and purpose – so that the process feels as rewarding as the celebration itself.

Chapter 8
Celebration Alchemiser

Mastering the Practice of Intentional Energy and Design

Welcome to your role as Celebration Alchemiser – bringing the Spirit of Celebration to life through presence, clarity and heart. This is Celebration Alchemistry: where energy meets event organising.

While logistics are important, this is an invitation to go beyond: to connect with the energetic and emotional core of the event. Because every intentional gathering has a heartbeat – a distinct energy that influences everything before, during and after. And that energy begins with you.

> *"People will forget what you said, people will forget what you did,*
> *but people will never forget how you made them feel."* – Maya Angelou

That feeling doesn't happen by accident. But let's be honest, when you're running on fumes, it's hard to hold energy well. You start with good intentions, then become knee-deep in logistics: guest lists, suppliers, endless questions. Soon, you're making it all happen while disappearing from your own experience.

To design differently, we first need to understand the energy we bring to every event – how our mindset and emotional state colour what we create.

The Paradigm Shift

Celebration 2.0 offers a shift from hustle to heart. A way of designing that centres meaning, energy and connection. This becomes your signature approach, what clients and others feel, even if they can't name it.

From Insight to Impact: Organising from SOUL

You've explored your patterns and energy in celebration. Now we move from celebrating well to designing celebration well – from participant to practitioner.

This new way of being and organising – aligning who you are with how you create – is built on two key upgrades at the heart of this book:

❖ **Life Mixology 1.0 to 2.0:** From autopilot reactivity to SOUL-aligned presence.

❖ **Celebration 1.0 to 2.0:** From pressure and performance to Purpose and Possibility.

As a Celebration Alchemiser, you hold the full arc: vision, energy, emotion and logistics. You bring intention to both your inner state and the outer experience you're creating.

Where Are You Coming from Right Now?

Before exploring organising styles, take a quick pause to check your energy. How you arrive directly affects how you organise and lead. This check-in uses the two key operating states – EGO and SOUL – and a critical quality for organisers: FLOW, the active expression of being aligned. Think of them as your internal compass for design and leadership decisions.

✑ **Organiser State Check-In™**

Purpose: Ground yourself before planning, leading or stepping into an event space.

When to use: Before client meetings, when prep feels overwhelming, mid-event when pressure rises, post-event debrief.

EGO State (Excessive, Grasping, Overthinking)

→ *Feels like:* Controlling every detail, seeking validation, racing to fix everything.

→ *Check-in:* Am I trying to control the outcome or create the experience?

SOUL State (Self-Aware, Open-Hearted, Unique, Legacy-Focused)

> → *Feels like:* Anchored in your "why," clear on what truly matters.

> → *Check-in:* Am I designing from my deepest values and vision for this event?

> And Am I in **FLOW?** (Flexible, Light, Optimistic, Willing)

> → *Feels like:* Responsive to what's emerging, creative under pressure.

> → *Check-in:* Can I adapt when things shift? What might be possible if I let curiosity lead?

Now that you've checked in with your current energy, let's look at the deeper patterns that influence how you plan, lead and respond under pressure.

Your Celebration Organising Style™

Each of us has a natural organising approach. When aligned, things flow, clarity arrives and energy becomes contagious. When stressed, old scripts and survival strategies take over, you find yourself in "Zilla Zone." This is you operating in "Zilla Mode" – that reactive, pressured state where you lose presence and forget your purpose. Think Bridezilla, Groomzilla, or any version of over-controlling, perfectionist, or shut-down organiser energy. It's your EGO's default pattern under stress.

Each Zilla Mode has a SOUL FLOW counterpart: your "Alchemiser Archetype" – who you are when you're aligned, intentional and leading from your strengths.

Organising Style: *your impact depends on whether you're operating from Zilla Mode or Alchemiser Archetype.*

A quick note on language:

I deliberately refer to Zilla as a *Mode* and Alchemiser as an *Archetype*. Zilla Mode is reactive and temporary; Archetype is your innate leadership energy and strengths.

I use "celebration" and "event" interchangeably; they both mean gathering experiences.

How to use the profiles ahead

Start by scanning the overview table to get a feel for your Organising Style. Then read the example (Type 6) to see how a profile comes to life. From there, explore the profiles to understand your patterns in more depth.

The goal isn't perfection – it's awareness. Follow what resonates; over time, you'll begin to recognise your own blend. When you do, you'll find it easier to shift from reactive *(Zilla Mode)* to intentional *(Alchemiser Archetype)* more quickly.

The Nine Organising Styles Overview

Type	Zilla Mode	Alchemiser Archetype
Type 1: The Reformer	**The Detail Tyrant** Perfection-obsessed, overly critical	**The Purposeful Composer** Clear, composed, guided by integrity
Type 2: The Giver	**The Party Martyr** Over-giving, boundary-blurring	**The Connection Curator** Heart-led, caring, emotionally attuned
Type 3: The Achiever	**The Glam Slam Chaser** Image-driven, high-performing	**The Impact Stylist** Dynamic, purposeful, engaged
Type 4: The Individualist	**The Mood Monarch** Emotional, sensitive, withdrawn	**The Sentiment Impressionist** Deep, expressive, creatively attuned
Type 5: The Observer	**The Intel Guard** Detached, over-analytical, hoards	**The Sovereign Essentialist** Wise, aligned, insightful
Type 6: The Loyalist	**The Compulsive Panic Prepper** Anxious, control-seeking	**The Steady Navigator** Calm, prepared, reassuring
Type 7: The Enthusiast	**The Glitter Bomber** Scattered, overstimulated	**The Joy Promoter** Playful, energising, visionary, present
Type 8: The Challenger	**The Event Overlord** Controlling, dominating	**The Gathering Guardian** Strong, steady, empowering
Type 9: The Peacemaker	**The Vanilla Blender** Avoidant, indecisive	**The Essence Harmoniser** Balanced, inclusive, unifying

Example: Type 6 in Action

Zilla Mode – *The Compulsive Panic Prepper:* You're organising a weekend wedding. Storms forecast. You've hired two marquees, printed waterproof programmes, added umbrellas to welcome bags. You arrive at dawn, frantic, emergency kit overflowing. You race through the day, scanning for problems, barely pausing to breathe. It's over. You've pulled it off, but you're strung out, too exhausted to savour or celebrate success.

SOUL Mode – *The Steady Navigator:* Same wedding, different energy. You arrive in plenty of time, coffee in hand and space to smile and connect. You've prepared and delegated. When plans shift, you're ready. Your calm sets the tone; guests and vendors feel safe. You stay energised and engaged throughout the day, noticing and acknowledging great support and service. At the end, you pause to savour how well it all came together – and to genuinely celebrate that feeling.

Your Alchemising Cocktail™

Your Alchemising Cocktail is your complete energetic profile as an organiser – a powerful self-awareness tool that helps you notice your habits, know your strengths and see your blind spots.

It brings together the four mixes we explored earlier:

- ❖ **Signature Mix** – Your core energy and patterns (who you are at baseline)

- ❖ **Celebration Cocktail** – The vibe you intend, or assume, you bring (how you prepare internally)

- ❖ **Co-Celebration Style** – How others experience you (your relational impact)

- ❖ **Organising Style** – How you plan, lead and create flow (your professional approach)

Together, these layers form your complete profile as an organiser – because how you show up personally directly influences how you lead professionally.

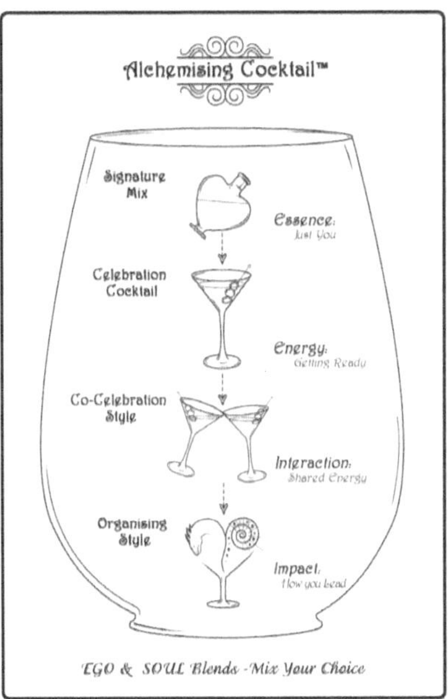

Alchemising Cocktail: Your complete energetic profile as an organiser.

Alchemising Cocktail Mixes – Nine blends inspired by the Enneagram

Now that you've met your four mixes, here's how they come alive together through nine unique Enneagram-inspired blends. These aren't deep analyses, just light-touch snapshots to give you a feel for what's at play – and what might be possible for you in your role (and in your life).

Take a sip of each one, notice what resonates or repels, and use that awareness to refine your own mix. The aim isn't to fix anything, but to bring more ease, presence and alignment to how you organise and lead.

Type 1: The Perfectionist

- ❖ **Zilla Mode:** The Detail Tyrant
- ❖ **Alchemising Archetype:** The Purposeful Composer

EGO Mix: Inner Perfectionism + Control Freak Cosmo + Celebration Critic + The Detail Tyrant

- → **Triggers:** Disorganisation, low standards, things done carelessly or without integrity
- → **Pattern:** Trying to perfect or control to force flow, becoming inflexible, silently judgemental.

SOUL Mix: Purposeful Precision + Let-It-Go Limoncello Spritz + Detail Hero + The Purposeful Composer

- → **Gift:** Brings order with ease, precision with purpose
- → *Reflection: What's already working? Focus on meaning and value, not what's wrong.*

Type 2: The Giver

- ❖ **Zilla Mode:** The Party Martyr
- ❖ **Alchemising Archetype:** The Connection Curator

EGO Mix: Over-Attuned + People-Pleaser Punch + Over-Attender + The Party Martyr

- → **Triggers:** Feeling unappreciated, having their support rejected or being excluded
- → **Pattern:** Overattending to everyone else, neglecting self, building resentment.

SOUL Mix: Heartfelt Generosity + Overflowing Love Bellini + Glow Guide + The Connection Curator

- → **Gift:** Creates warmth and belonging, giving with ease and receiving with grace
- → *Reflection: What would nourish you now? When you honour your own needs, your connection is authentic and alive.*

Type 3: The Achiever

- ❖ **Zilla Mode:** The Glam Slam Chaser
- ❖ **Alchemising Archetype:** The Impact Stylist

EGO Mix: Image-Fuelled Drive + Trophy Espresso Martini + Spotlight Seeker + The Glam Slam Chaser

- → **Triggers:** Feeling overlooked, flat energy, lack of momentum
- → **Pattern:** Overproducing to impress, forgetting the heart of the moment.

SOUL Mix: Authentic Radiance + True Joy Gimlet + Wow Spotlighter + The Impact Stylist

- → **Gift:** Inspires through authentic energy and bold vision
- → ***Reflection:*** *What feels true right now? Lead from the heart, not highlight reel performance.*

Type 4: The Individualist

- ❖ **Zilla Mode:** The Mood Monarch
- ❖ **Alchemising Archetype:** The Sentiment Impressionist

EGO Mix: Emotional Intensity + Melancholy Merlot + Air Kisser + The Mood Monarch

- → **Triggers:** Feeling unseen, surface-level moments, lack of emotional depth in an experience
- → **Pattern:** Chasing meaning instead of living it, creating intensity but feeling apart even when present.

SOUL Mix: Soulful Clarity + Vibrant Sangria + Depth Whisperer + The Sentiment Impressionist

- → **Gift:** Creates experiences that touch hearts, turns moments into memories
- → ***Reflection:*** *What's genuine and moving right now? Joy doesn't need depth to be felt.*

Type 5: The Observer

❖ **Zilla Mode:** The Intel Guard

❖ **Alchemising Arche**type: The Sovereign Essentialist

EGO Mix: Withheld Presence + Energy-Saver Negroni + Silent Witness + The Intel Guard

→ **Triggers:** Too much small talk, crowded energy, pressure to perform, chaotic spaces

→ **Pattern:** Present but not available, watching from the sidelines, keeping distance, conserving energy.

SOUL Mix: Calm Enquirer + Curious Clover Club + Quiz Master + The Sovereign Essentialist

→ **Gift:** Brings clarity and calm wisdom, designs thoughtful, well-paced experiences

→ *Reflection: Where might you be holding back? Wisdom grows when shared.*

Type 6: The Loyalist

❖ **Zilla Mode:** The Compulsive Panic Prepper

❖ **Alchemising Arche**type: The Steady Navigator

EGO Mix: Vigilance Spiral + Anxiety on the Rocks + Barcoder + The Compulsive Panic Prepper

→ **Triggers:** Uncertainty, last-minute changes, unclear plans, chaotic collaborators

→ **Pattern:** Overpreparing for risk, scanning for problems, losing sight of what's flowing well.

SOUL Mix: Grounded Assurance + Trust-the-Moment Mojito + Flow Forti-fier + The Steady Navigator

> → **Gift:** Steadies the ship, helps others feel at ease through thoughtful preparation

> → *Reflection: What's actually needed right now? Trust doesn't mean ignoring risk, just easing control.*

Type 7: The Enthusiast

❖ **Zilla Mode:** The Glitter Bomber

❖ **Alchemising Archetype:** The Joy Promoter

EGO Mix: Scattered Stimulation + FOMO Fireball Daiquiri + Social Butterfly + The Glitter Bomber

> → **Triggers:** Rejected ideas, repetitive formats, creativity being curtailed

> → **Pattern:** Overloading experiences to keep energy high, becoming overstimulated, losing focus and meaning.

SOUL Mix: Joyful Calm + Fully Present Passionfruit Martini + Vibe Magi-cian + The Joy Promoter

> → **Gift:** Brings infectious energy and bright ideas, turning creativity into shared delight

> → *Reflection: What atmosphere are you creating? Joy spreads when energy is steady, not scattered.*

Type 8: The Challenger

❖ **Zilla Mode:** The Event Overlord

❖ **Alchemising Archetype:** The Gathering Guardian

EGO Mix: Intense Core + Power Play Whiskey Sour + Demander + The Event Overlord

→ **Triggers:** Feeling disrespected, vulnerable, or out of control, indecision or lack of direction

→ **Pattern:** Taking control to shut others down, turning collaboration into power play.

SOUL Mix: Open Strength + Full-hearted Old Fashioned + Inclusive Ally + The Gathering Guardian

→ **Gift:** Holds the room with confidence, creating safety for others to stand tall

→ *Reflection: How can your strength invite others in? Openness is the mark of authentic power.*

Type 9: The Peacemaker

❖ **Zilla Mode:** The Vanilla Blender

❖ **Alchemising Archetype:** The Essence Harmoniser

EGO Mix: Comfortable Disconnection + Go-With-the-Flow Fizz + Peace Zoner + The Vanilla Blender

→ **Triggers:** Tension, conflict, unclear direction, being asked to take sides

→ **Pattern:** Avoiding decisions, prioritising calm over clarity, blending in instead of guiding through tension.

SOUL Mix: Embodied Harmony + Happy Highball + Ease Connector + The Essence Harmoniser

> → **Gift:** Unifies without losing self, designs and holds space with ease and flow to bring calm cohesion

> → *Reflection: How might you show up more fully? True harmony needs whole presence.*

Your Alchemising Cocktail in Play

To recap:

> → Use this information to build awareness, not to label or judge yourself or others.

> → Think of it as a mirror, a guide, and perhaps a conversation starter.

> → Keep checking your blend. It's uniquely yours, and it will evolve with time, attention and intention.

> → Notice your patterns – especially what pulls you into Zilla Mode and consider how you can lead from your Archetype instead.

> → When your behaviour drifts, pause and reflect. What part of your mix is in play?

> → When things flow, take time to notice which aspects of your mix supported that success.

Every time you pause, notice and realign, you strengthen your alchemical muscle. You become more conscious in how you create, lead and influence. That's the real work of a Celebration Alchemiser – influencing experiences not just through plans and processes, but through presence, intention and heart.

Your Energy Is Your Legacy

Every celebration leaves an energetic imprint. Your presence as an organiser carries weight; people remember the feeling you create. That's where your legacy – and your reputation – live. Things won't always go to plan.

When something feels off, awareness is everything. Pause and ask: *Where am I coming from right now – Zilla or Archetype? Use 5Alive as a guide:*

→ Am I *A*ligned?

→ Am I *L*ive (present)?

→ Am I *I*ntentional?

→ Am I *V*ital (joyful)?

→ What's my *E*nergy like?

Awareness gives you choice. And choice is where alchemy begins.

The Alchemiser's Studio

This is your creative sanctuary – the space, literal or metaphorical, where you step back from logistics and energetically step into purpose and vision. It's where you move from managing an event to designing an experience.

The Alchemiser's Studio: Your creative space where purpose, vision, intention and energy meet to design meaningful experiences.

In your Studio:

> → Purpose expands into vision

> → Energy grounds in intention

> → Intuition enlivens frameworks

> → Alchemy adds magic and meaning to the experience.

Think of it as the difference between a bartender at their service station – functional, reactive, pouring drinks on demand – and a master mixologist in a creative lab – imaginative, experimental, crafting something extraordinary. Both are essential, but only one invites something deeper: connection, creativity and transformation.

Your Studio is where awareness and alignment happen. It's where you work with your **Alchemising Cocktail** – your unique blend and organising presence – to understand it more deeply and consciously choose how you mix and pour it.

The Studio is also where intuitive hits meet practical planning and where the question shifts from *What needs to happen? to What wants to emerge?* Here, personal insight and creative design come together, influencing not only how you lead but how each experience unfolds.

Your Studio doesn't have to be a physical place. It's the space where you step into your Alchemising energy – the inner state that connects purpose and possibility. It might begin with your initial brainstorming, but you'll return to it throughout the process: in a moment between meetings when you need perspective or when you need calm before an event goes live.

What matters is the energy you bring, crossing that threshold from reactive planning to intentional creation, from performance to presence, from logistics to alignment with purpose and vision.

Every return to your Studio – every intentional immersion in your Alchemising energy – steadily builds your personal and professional legacy.

You're not working alone in this space. The Spirit of Celebration is right there with you – guiding, nudging, sometimes stirring things up to help you see more clearly. When you open to her presence, you begin to notice a subtle pull at work. It's called Creative Tension.

Working with Creative Tension

Understanding this concept will serve you well as an organiser.

Every act of creation, every idea being brought to life, carries a stretch – it's the dynamic tension between where you are now (current reality) and where you want to be (vision). This tension may feel uncomfortable, but it's alive with potential. This is where the "not yet" lives – the space where purpose begins to take shape. Don't rush to fix it or force an answer. Stay with it – stay curious and open. That's where insight and inspiration live. That's your creative fuel.

Alongside the unseen presence of the Spirit of Celebration, you have practical tools and frameworks to help you lead and design with greater intention. You'll find these within what I call your Oracle – your go-to resource as a Celebration Alchemiser. We'll explore this next.

Chapter 9
Your Alchemising Oracle –
SOUL Leadership in Action

In Chapter 8, you discovered your Celebration Organising Style and the two very different energies you bring when you're in EGO Zilla Mode or SOUL FLOW Archetype – part of your full energetic profile, your Alchemising Cocktail. But insight alone isn't enough.

Your energy becomes your legacy. It determines how people experience you, not just in what you design, but in how you lead, respond and show up throughout the entire process.

Your Oracle is your guide to using your energy intentionally, supporting you as you lead by example in how you design, deliver and close every experience. It's your real-time companion for navigating pressure, shifting your state and returning to presence.

Your Oracle at a Glance

Think of your Oracle not as a manual or workbook, but as a reference guide. A daily touchstone to help you return to the version of yourself that leads with presence, even when things get unpredictable or intense.

It's organised into four layers, from foundation to refinement:

→ FOUNDATION: Your Alchemising A-Game (5-step daily compass)

→ DEEPENING: Your Alchemising Cocktail (understanding your patterns)

→ EXPANSION: The Alchemiser's Arts (5 creative intelligence tools)

→ REFINEMENT: Your Alchemiser's Stances (5 conscious perspectives)

You don't need to master it all at once. Start with A-Game as your foundation, then deepen as you're ready. Dip in when you need support, or return time and again to strengthen your practice.

How to Use This Oracle

→ **Start** with the A-Game. The 5 steps (Arrive, Assess, Align, Activate, Anchor) are your core practice. Use them daily until they become second nature.

→ **When you're ready to deepen:** Add your Cocktail awareness. Understand your Zilla triggers and Alchemiser gifts. This helps you shift faster.

→ **To expand your creative range:** Explore the Arts. These are innate capabilities you already have – you're just naming and refining them.

→ **For specific challenges:** Use the Stances. They're conscious perspectives for situations where you need a specific lens.

→ **Bottom line:** A-Game is your foundation. Everything else enriches it, but you don't need it all to lead well. What matters most is being intentional and self-aware – that's what will keep you growing.

FOUNDATION: **Your Alchemising A-Game**

Your daily leadership compass

Your "A-Game" is your five-part leadership formula. It's how you show up with clarity, care and creative presence, no matter your role or what's happening around you. It helps you take responsibility for your energy and lead with intention rather than react from stress or habit.

The A-Game Core Practice: five steps to recalibrate in real-time:

- ❖ **Arrive** (presence) – Internal scan

- ❖ **Assess** (clarity) – External scan

- ❖ **Align** (intention) – Reconnect with purpose

- ❖ **Activate** (purposeful action) – Engage mindfully

- ❖ **Anchor** (completion and integration) – Close and reset

You can think of these as steps or practices that guide how you respond to what's happening within and around you. They can be used sequentially, or you might find that focusing on just one is enough in the moment. With practice, it becomes second nature. You'll instinctively know which move will bring the most clarity and impact.

- ❖ **Step 1: Arrive**

What it is: An internal scan to ground yourself in the present moment

Purpose: Presence. Before you can respond wisely, you need to land here, now – not spiralling into worst-case scenarios or racing ahead to solutions.

What this invites: Pause. Breathe. Feel your feet on the ground. Come back to your body, to this moment, to what's actually here.

Key Questions:

- → *Am I actually here, or already three steps ahead?*

- → *Can I take one full breath before I react?*

- → *What would it feel like to simply be present right now?*

❖ **Step 2: Assess**

What it is: Read the situation clearly

Purpose: Clarity. Now that you're present, what's actually happening? Not your story about it, not your fear – just the facts and the full picture.

What this invites: Observe without judgement. See what you might be missing when your nervous system is activated. Let information land before you interpret it.

Key Questions:

→ *What are the actual facts here?*

→ *What am I making this mean that might not be true?*

→ *What else is happening that I'm not yet seeing?*

❖ **Step 3: Align**

What it is: An internal decision to reconnect with what matters.

Purpose: Intention. This is your leadership choice point, a moment to decide how you want to move forward. Alignment means anchoring your decisions in what's truly important instead of getting swept up in distractions, hidden agendas or anxiety.

What this invites: Focus on what's important to you. Make a clear, calm choice about your next step.

Key Questions:

→ *What actually matters right now?*

→ *What choice aligns with my values and bigger purpose?*

→ *How might I let go of fear and trust that clarity will come as I move with intention?*

❖ Step 4: Activate

What it is: External action – choosing to engage mindfully.

Purpose: Purposeful Action. Your presence influences the moment far beyond logistics. This is where thoughtful intention facilitates mindful engagement and focused direction.

What this invites: Take deliberate action that reflects your alignment. Move with purpose and stay aware and responsive to real-time shifts in energy, people and plans.

Key Questions:

→ *What action would best serve the experience and the bigger picture?*

→ *How might I bring presence and care to what I do next?*

→ *How might I trust my instincts and lead from the heart right now?*

❖ Step 5: Anchor

What it is: Internal reflection to close and reset.

Purpose: Completion and integration. This is about appreciation and learning. Which only happens when we create space to pause, acknowledge and integrate what has happened, so you can close this "chapter" fully and prepare for the next. Without this reflection, insights slip away and old habits repeat and reinforce themselves.

What this invites: Think of it as an energetic exhale. Sometimes it's a breath and a moment of quiet. Other times, it's a deeper or formal review of what shifted, what was achieved and what still needs attention.

Key Questions:

→ *What needs to be acknowledged before moving on?*

→ *What has been learned that can be carried forward?*

→ *How might we honour what has been and welcome what's coming next?*

A-Game in Practice: The Venue Mix-Up

To help you see how the A-Game plays out in real life, let's walk through a scenario.

The Situation: You've just received a voicemail from a venue manager: they've double-booked your client's event and cancelled at the last minute. Your heart's racing. And you have a big pitch in ten minutes, a meeting you can't afford to blow.

Default Response (EGO): Panic floods your system. Your mind races with catastrophic thoughts. You want to shout, slam your desk. You fire off an angry voicemail, your team picks up the friction, and you enter the pitch with jagged energy. The presentation is technically polished, but your presence is off. The pitch falls flat.

A-Game Response (SOUL FLOW):

Arrive: You feel the panic rising, but you pause and breathe. You notice your heart pounding, the urge to explode, but you don't let it run you. You create space to respond rather than react.

Assess: You step back and see the full picture. Yes, there's a crisis, but there's also an opportunity right in front of you. Your main priority is landing this client. You won't let the venue disaster derail your pitch.

Align: You remind yourself of the bigger picture, the *why* behind what you do. You choose to address the crisis quickly to free up headspace for what matters most right now.

Activate: You send a calm, professional email to the venue with the confirmation attached. Your tone is open and non-accusatory. You request a meeting for later that day. Then you turn your full attention to the pitch, gathering your team with clear, centred energy.

Anchor: After the pitch, you take a moment to reflect. You acknowledge the stress you felt and the calm you chose when it mattered. You follow up on the venue situation with centred energy, and when you do land the client, you celebrate with your team, knowing your presence made the difference.

The Shift: Same facts, different energy. Leadership through presence, not pressure.

DEEPENING: **Your Alchemising Cocktail in Leadership**

Understanding and adjusting your energetic impact

You explored your complete Alchemising Cocktail in Chapter 8 – the four layers that make up your energetic signature as an organiser. Here's how to use it as a real-time leadership tool.

Quick Reminder: Your Cocktail Components

- ❖ **Signature Mix:** Your baseline energy
- ❖ **Celebration Cocktail:** The energy you intend or assume you bring
- ❖ **Co-Celebration Style:** How others experience you
- ❖ **Organising Style:** Your approach under pressure (Zilla Mode vs Alchemiser Archetype)

Integrating Your Cocktail with A-Game

When pressure's on, your A-Game helps you pause and choose your next move. Your Cocktail adds depth by showing you *what* to notice at each step:

A-Game Step	Cocktail Check-In	Leadership Focus	Key Question
Arrive	Signature Mix	Pause and notice your internal state (EGO or SOUL)	What energy am I in right now? What flavour is dominant?
Assess	Co-Celebration Style	Observe the room and what's unfolding	What vibe am I adding? What cues can I pick up from the space?
Align	Celebration Cocktail	Reconnect with what matters	What energy do I want to bring now? What needs adjusting?
Activate	Organising Style	Take intentional, purposeful action	Am I acting from presence or pressure? What's my focus and next priority?
Anchor	Full mix	Reflect, learn and reset	What played out in my blend? What helped and what felt off?

Remember: You're not trying to fix yourself. You're learning to lead from awareness, not habit. The Cocktail gives you language, insight and options, especially when things get challenging.

Your A-Game keeps you steady. Your Alchemising Cocktail keeps you aligned. Together, they help you deepen your leadership and build your legacy.

EXPANSION: **The Alchemiser's Arts**

Your creative intelligence superpowers

As a Celebration Alchemiser, you're working with presence, energy and emergence. The five Alchemiser's Arts – **Imagination, Intuition, Open Curiosity, Zenergy,** and **Visioning** – are innate capabilities you already possess. They are your creative intelligence in action:

❖ Imagination – *Where wonder opens possibility*

What it is: Your ability to dream beyond what is, to picture what could be, even if you're not sure how to get there. This isn't wild ideas for the sake of it. It's giving yourself permission to play with possibility – to go beyond rational thinking and reconnect with wonder.

In practice: Seeing potential in an awkward venue and turning it into magic. Daring to ask, *What if we could do this differently?*

Leadership edge: Breaks the mould of "same old" thinking and opens fresh possibilities.

❖ Intuition – *Where instinct whispers wisdom*

What it is: That quiet nudge, that knowing feeling in your gut that something's off or just right. It's not logic or guesswork. It's deep sensing that helps you move faster, calmer and with greater precision.

In practice: Pause before saying yes. Shifting room energy with a well-timed question. Knowing something needs simplifying, even if you can't explain why.

Leadership edge: Greater clarity and creativity, with faster decisions and less overthinking.

❖ Open Curiosity – *Where innocence makes room for insight*

What it is: The part of you that stays open, even under pressure. It chooses wonder over worry, questions over assumptions. It keeps your leadership human and your choices responsive, not reactive.

In practice: Asking *What else could be true here?* Letting someone surprise you. Pausing to see what's actually needed rather than solving the wrong problem.

Leadership edge: Inclusive and open leadership that encourages innovation.

❖ **Zenergy** – *Where emotion fuels wise action*

What it is: Your emotional intelligence in motion. It's how you read a room, feel the pulse and move with your emotions, without being run by them. You don't avoid or suppress them. You ride them with awareness.

In practice: Noticing your tension and softening your tone instead of raising your voice. Harnessing excitement to lift a room. Holding space for someone who needs to be seen.

Leadership edge: Presence that influences positive outcomes and creates emotional safety.

❖ **Visioning** – *Where all the Arts converge*

What it is: Visioning is the point where all the arts work together. It's how the big picture begins to take form. Here, insights and ideas are gathered, connected and given direction, so that the abstract becomes tangible and momentum builds around a shared vision.

In practice: It's sensing what's ready to emerge and making space to guide it into being – into something that others can see and build on. That moment when an idea clicks and the whole team lights up with fresh creativity.

Leadership edge: Creating alignment around shared possibility, inviting collaborations and letting solutions emerge naturally.

❖ **When Arts Align: Inspiration**

When you're fully immersed in your Alchemising energy – especially in your Studio space – something deeper can arise: a quiet moment when everything clicks and your whole being says **yes, this**. You can't force or plan it, but you can make space for it by being open, curious, present and patient. The word *inspire* means "to breathe in spirit," and that's often when Celly slips in with a nudge of clarity, joy and possibility. Bringing the heart and soul to your celebration – the quiet kind of magic that reminds you why you do this, and why it matters.

Arts Activation Quick-Hits – *Micro-practices for busy moments*

> → **Imagination:** "What if …?" + 2-minute brainstorm

> → **Intuition:** Pause, breathe, sense; what does your gut say?

> → **Open Curiosity:** "What else might be true here?"

> → **Zenergy:** Feel the energetic pulse, breathe, ground in presence

> → **Visioning:** Drop logic and pause to sense "What wants to emerge through this situation?"

REFINEMENT: Your Alchemiser's Stances

Five conscious perspectives you adopt for specific challenges

The Stances are *situational lenses* – conscious perspectives you choose based on what a specific moment needs. Where the Arts are always with you, the Stances are what you step into. You'll see each one applied in the next chapter through the five-step intentional design framework, SPARK.

❖ **The Purposeful Architect** – Grounded in meaning, guided by intention

When to use: Team loses sight of *why,* energy is scattered, or everyone's locked in logistics.

What it brings: Reconnection with the deeper purpose and intention.

Key move: "What's the real purpose here? What did we say this needs to set in motion?"

In practice: In a design session spiralling into surface details, you pause and ask about the bigger picture. The energy shifts, the room resets, fixing and rational thinking fall away and true design begins.

❖ **The Intuitive Artist** – Tuned into energy, led by insight

When to use: Something feels missing; logic alone won't get you there; you need to sense the bigger picture and what's at play beneath the surface.

What it brings: Connection to the vibe, what wants to emerge.

Key move: "What's the spirit we're missing? Where's the part people will connect with?"

In practice: Reviewing a polished plan that feels flat, you name what's missing, the heart of it. Your reframing helps others sense it too, and fresh ideas surface.

❖ **The Truth Seeker** – Guided by honesty and compassion

When to use: When there's an elephant in the room, or difficult conversations are being avoided, or when something feels off.

What it brings: Clarity through compassionate honesty.

Key move: Name what's real with kindness and directness.

In practice: When a team member inappropriately nominates themselves for a role, you address it calmly and clearly, allowing everyone to reset without shame or blame.

❖ **The Goldsmith** – Refining for alignment

When to use: Something's off, but you can't pinpoint what, flow is stalled or feels clunky.

What it brings: Ability to spot and adjust what's out of sync.

Key move: "What small adjustment would make this flow better?"

In practice: Reviewing a run sheet that's technically solid but doesn't feel right, you identify subtle refinements – more breathing space, cleaner transitions – that let the experience land more spaciously and effectively.

❖ **The Legacy Holder** – Honouring what lasts

When to use: Lost in logistics, missing meaning and memory, closing moments.

What it brings: Long-term view and connection to what needs to live on.

Key move: "What do we want this to mean? What stays with people afterwards?"

In practice: Reviewing a company's anniversary celebration that's technically perfect but missing the vitality that makes its legacy felt; you ask when people actually get to experience that connection. Together, you weave in stories, gratitude and moments that honour the journey.

INTEGRATION: From Practice to Mastery

You've explored the four layers of your Oracle: A-Game for daily recalibration, Cocktail for energetic awareness, Arts for creative intelligence, and Stances for conscious perspective. These aren't new skills to master – they're innate capabilities you're learning to use more intentionally. The question now is: how do you bring this inner alignment into the design itself? How does presence become creation that leaves a lasting impact?

That's where the SPARK Synergy Framework comes in. Chapter 10 opens the SPARK design process, where your Alchemising energy finds expression and your true role as a Celebration Alchemiser fully unfolds.

QUICK REFERENCE: Oracle Tools

This is a handy guide for real-time recalibration when you need to quickly ground, reset or choose your next move with clarity and calm.

⟋ Your Oracle at a Glance

Priority	Framework	Quick Description	When to Use	Core Aspects
Start Here (foundation)	**Alchemising A-Game**	5-step leadership recalibration	Daily pressure moments	❖ Arrive ❖ Assess ❖ Align ❖ Activate ❖ Anchor
Deepen:	**Alchemising Cocktail**	Your energetic signature	Understanding your patterns, blind spots, growth path	❖ Signature Mix ❖ Celebration Cocktail ❖ Co-Celebration Style ❖ Organising Style
Expand:	**Alchemiser's Arts**	Creative intelligence toolkit	When logic isn't enough	❖ Imagination ❖ Intuition ❖ Open Curiosity ❖ Zenergy ❖ Visioning
Refine:	**Alchemiser's Stances**	Conscious perspectives	Guiding specific situations	❖ Purposeful Architect ❖ Intuitive Artist ❖ Truth Seeker ❖ Goldsmith ❖ Legacy Holder

✎ A-Game Prompt Cards

- ❖ **Arrive Card:**

  ⇨ Pause. Breathe.

  ⇨ What energy am I bringing?

  ⇨ Notice without fixing.

- ❖ **Assess Card:**

  ⇨ Step back. Observe.

  ⇨ What's really happening here?

  ⇨ What might I be missing?

- ❖ **Align Card:**

  ⇨ What actually matters?

  ⇨ What choice serves the bigger picture?

  ⇨ Where's my true north?

- ❖ **Activate Card:**

  ⇨ How can I engage with presence?

  ⇨ What action aligns with my intention?

  ⇨ Stay open to real-time shifts.

- ❖ **Anchor Card:**

  ⇨ What needs acknowledging?

  ⇨ What have I learned?

  ⇨ How do I want to close this chapter?

⟋ Cocktail Integration Table

When You Notice...	Check This	Ask Yourself
Feeling scattered or reactive	Signature Mix	What's my baseline right now?
Others seeming disconnected	Co-Celebration Style	How am I engaging with people?
Energy feeling misaligned	Celebration Cocktail	What energy do I want to bring? What's getting in the way?
Slipping into control mode	Organising Style	Am I leading from presence (Archetype) or pressure (Zilla Mode)?

⟋ Arts Quick Activators

→ **Stuck in logic?** Call in Imagination: *What if ...?*

→ **Overthinking decisions?** Trust Intuition: Pause, breathe, sense.

→ **Rushing to conclusions?** Open Curiosity: *What else might be true?*

→ **Disconnected from feeling?** Zenergy: Embody good energy, adjust presence.

→ **Lost in details?** Visioning: Suspend logic: *What wants to emerge here?*

⟋ Stance Quick Selector

> → **Team unfocused?** Purposeful Architect: *What's our real purpose?*
>
> → **Something feels flat?** Intuitive Artist: *Where's the spirit?*
>
> → **Avoiding difficult truths?** Truth Seeker: Name what's real with care.
>
> → **Flow feels off?** Goldsmith: *What needs refining?*
>
> → **Missing the meaning?** Legacy Holder: *What do we want this to mean?*

This Oracle is your companion for the journey ahead. Return to it whenever you need to reconnect with your centre, recalibrate your presence or remember the leader you came here to be.

Chapter 10
SPARK Synergy

Strategic, Intentional Celebration Design

You've got your A-Game on. Your studio is open. You've tapped into your creative intelligence and leadership presence. Now you get to embrace your alchemising role more fully through intentional design. Welcome to SPARK – five intentional steps for meaningful experience design.

SPARK Synergy Framework™

> **S** – Set Purpose and Intention
>
> **P** – Paint the Vision
>
> **A** – Assess the Current Reality
>
> **R** – Realign Actions
>
> **K** – Keep Legacy

SPARK isn't your standard event planning framework. It's a soulful design process that begins before the logistics, guiding how you work with the energy, purpose and emotional truth of what you're creating. Whether you're designing a wedding, hosting a workshop or even writing a book (yes, I used it for this one), SPARK gives you a clear path from vision to impact.

The events industry is shifting. Experience designers such as Tahira Endean have reminded us that powerful gatherings aren't just well-planned: they're intentionally designed and deeply felt. SPARK is my signature approach to this, blending heart with strategy, presence with purpose. At its core is the belief that celebration is more than logistics. It's a container for possibility.

SPARK Synergy Framework: Five steps for designing soul-aligned celebrations that blend heart, strategy and presence.

Along the way, you'll meet your patterns (hello, Zilla Zone) and learn how to realign yourself and the process. You'll lead through your Alchemiser Archetype, turning every celebration into an opportunity for meaningful transformation.

How SPARK Works

Each step has a **specific design focus** and draws on your Oracle tools:

❖ A **Stance** to guide your perspective

❖ **Arts** to activate your creative intelligence

❖ **Energy prompts** to stay grounded

You'll recognise these from Chapter 9. Now, we put them into practice within the design process itself. You'll find a handy overview of all this in the SPARK Synergy Framework table.

Throughout this chapter, you'll see each of these integrations come alive through one couple's celebration journey. The table will make more sense as you go – and you can return to it as a reference throughout your own SPARK practice.

SPARK Synergy Framework: Your Complete Reference Guide

Step	Design Focus (what you're doing)	Key Question (to ask yourself)	Alchemiser's Stance (perspective to take)	Energy Prompt (to embody)	Alchemising Arts (innate capabilities)
S: **Set Purpose and Intention**	**Clarify** Establish the purpose (why) and the intention (how it should feel and flow)	Why does this celebration matter? What energy will guide it?	*The Purposeful Architect* Cuts through noise with clarity	Anchor in SOUL FLOW	❖ Imagination ❖ Intuition ❖ Open Curiosity ❖ Zenergy ❖ Visioning
P: **Paint the Vision**	**Envision** Sense into the atmosphere, energy and moments that want to emerge	What might be possible if this celebration fully expressed its purpose and intention?	*The Intuitive Artist* Senses the look/feel before details decided	Breathe and invite images	
A: **Assess Current Reality**	**Diagnose** Check if your current direction is still aligned with your original purpose, intention and vision	What's off track, unclear, or no longer working and what might need to shift?	*The Truth Seeker* Pauses to see clearly, names the ignored obvious	Sit with Creative Tension	
R: **Realign Actions**	**Refocus** Redirect your efforts based on what's true, timely and aligned	What action would make the biggest difference right now?	*The Goldsmith* Refines and realigns	Move with clarity	
K: **Keep Legacy**	**Sustain** Design with intention for how the story and impact live on	What will live on after the event? What will be set in motion?	*The Legacy Holder* Focuses on what carries forward	Honour your energy	

Your Celebration Blueprint™: The Strategic Foundation

Before logistics you need a Blueprint.

Your Celebration Blueprint is your project's strategic foundation: the four core elements that define what this celebration is really about and why it matters. It's what keeps you grounded when a hundred decisions compete for attention.

Why It Matters

Most event planning starts with logistics: date, venue, guest count. But when you start there, you're building without a foundation. Details multiply, decisions feel arbitrary and the celebration risks becoming a well-executed event that doesn't actually move anyone or change anything.

The Blueprint solves this. It gives you:

> → **Clarity** on what truly matters (so you can say "no" to what doesn't)

> → **Alignment** across all decisions (so everything reinforces the same purpose)

> → **Confidence** when challenged (you know your "why")

> → **Meaning** that lasts (not just logistics that land)

How You Build and Use It Through SPARK

Your Blueprint develops progressively as you move through SPARK. It consists of four foundation elements (from Steps S,P and K). It becomes your constant reference point and realignment yardstick (Steps A and R). Here's how it works:

Step S – Set Purpose and Intention

You uncover the deeper *why* (Purpose) and define the guiding *energy* (Intention) through deep listening. These become your foundation.

Step P – Paint the Vision

You add the *big picture* (Vision) by sensing what wants to emerge. Now you can see where you're going.

Steps A and R – Assess and Realign

You use your Blueprint to check if you're still aligned and realign when you drift. It's your compass, not a static document.

Step K – Keep Legacy

You define the *lasting impact* (Legacy) from the beginning and you protect the Blueprint's integrity right through to delivery.

CELEBRATION BLUEPRINT

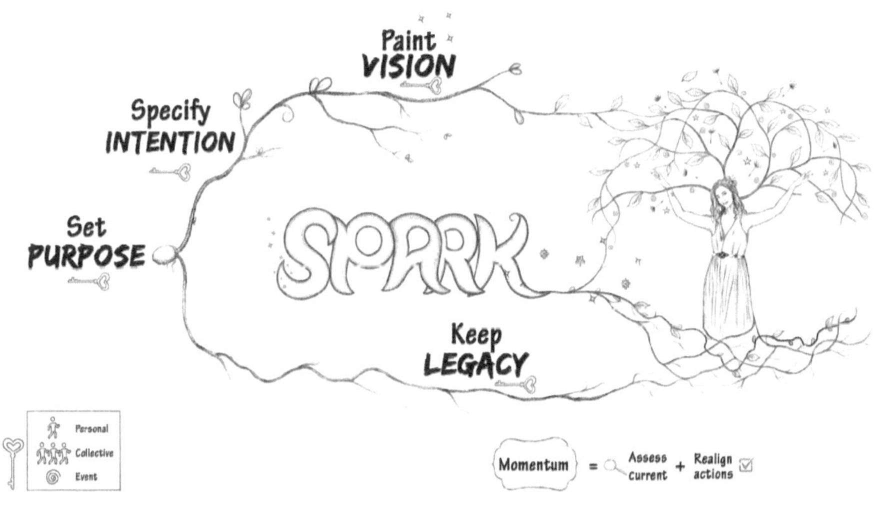

The Celebration Blueprint SPARK's elements as a living synergy that creates meaning and impact, inspired and aligned with Celly at the centre of the experience.

In Practice

Your Blueprint is a living document – not a one-time deliverable, it evolves as you go and acts as your constant reference point. Every decision runs through this filter:

> → Vendor pitches idea – "Does this serve our Purpose?"

> → Budget cuts needed – "What can we lose without compromising Intention?"

> → Timeline compresses – "What protects the Vision?"

> → Post-event choices – "Does this honour the Legacy we're building?"

The Blueprint isn't one more document to create. It's what prevents you from drowning in documents that don't prioritise the heart and soul of the experience.

Now let's see how you build it …

SPARK Synergy: When Energy, Intention and Design Come Together

SPARK Synergy is the multiplier effect that happens when intention and design meet essence and presence. It's the quiet magic that emerges when you work in partnership with Celly, our Spirit of Celebration, whose frequency holds joy, connection, appreciation, meaning and possibility.

At its heart, synergy is when the whole becomes greater than the sum of its parts. When energy, purpose and thoughtful design flow together, something more magnetic unfolds – something that resonates deeper, lands truer and lives longer. This is the source of legacy.

What SPARK Will Do for Your Practice

The Challenge: Events meant to connect often leave people drained, disconnected or disappointed. Despite perfect logistics, something essential gets lost – the soul of celebration.

The Solution: SPARK – a five-step process that adds soul to strategy, ensuring your events resonate and create lasting meaning alongside exceptional delivery.

The Results:

- Events that shift energy and create genuine connection

- Reduced planning burnout through aligned action

- Enhanced reputation as a transformational experience designer

- Personal fulfilment that sustains long-term career satisfaction

SPARK isn't here to replace your current systems; it enhances them.

→ **Steps S** and **P** come before the logistics, forming your Celebration Blueprint, your source of truth.

→ **Steps A** and **R** work in tandem with your systems, keeping you aware and intentional.

→ **Step K** is about building energy and legacy the whole way through.

SPARK sharpens focus, prevents planning fatigue and keeps your work energised and meaningful. It's what sets you apart as a Celebration Alchemiser. You're not just managing details. You're sensing into the deeper story and designing an experience that truly resonates.

SPARK is a journey of professional and personal transformation. Each step builds on the last, deepening your capacity to create experiences that resonate.

Your Energy Matters

Before you begin SPARK, check your state. Your energy affects every decision, conversation and outcome. Are you in Zilla Mode (rushed, controlling, over-perfecting) or your Alchemiser Archetype (grounded, present, open)?

⁄ **Quick 5Alive Check**

> → Aligned with your role and values?
>
> → Live (present, not overthinking)?
>
> → Intentional about your energy?
>
> → Vital (connected to joy and creativity)?
>
> → Energy steady (what do you need)?

Aligned organisers create aligned experiences.

SPARK Step S – Set Purpose and Intention

Start with meaning. Design from essence.

What This Step Does

Step S defines your event's two foundational elements:

> ❖ **Purpose:** The deeper *why* behind the celebration
>
> ❖ **Intention:** The guiding energy that brings that why to life

These become the cornerstone of your Celebration Blueprint.

Skipping this step leads to rushed, reactive planning. But when you begin here, everything that follows is anchored in depth and meaning. This is how you shift from surface-level logistics to soul-level design.

Start with Purpose

Purpose is the deeper why – the seed of the celebration. It's what makes the event matter, not just for today but for what it sets in motion – its legacy.

In *The Art of Gathering,* Priya Parker reminds us that purpose is not just a nice-to-have; it's foundational. That we should never start a gathering without knowing why we're doing it.

But don't assume the occasion itself gives you the purpose. That first reason – the surface label – is often just the starting point. "It's a wedding." "It's a team day." These are headlines, not the full story.

The real purpose usually sits quietly beneath, waiting to be uncovered. A wedding honours love, yes, but it may also weave together two families and cultures. A team day might celebrate progress, but at its heart could be about rebuilding trust and connection.

Name the Intention

Once you've clarified the deeper *why,* the next question is how to bring it into a lived experience. That's where intention comes in.

If purpose is the seed, intention is how you nurture it, through presence, energy and aligned choices. Where purpose zooms out, intention zooms in. It shapes how the celebration will feel and what it will evoke. Will it be joyful or superficial? Meaningful or mechanical? Nourishing or overwhelming?

Intention is what people experience. It's the energy that turns purpose into felt reality.

Purpose gives you direction. Intention brings it to life.

Three Layers of Purpose and Intention

To sketch a powerful Celebration Blueprint, we map purpose and intention across three interconnected layers: Personal, Relational and Event.

Personal Layer: Your motivation and energy as the organiser

❖ **Personal Purpose:** What you hope to bring, enable, or stand for

❖ **Personal Intention:** The quality of energy or presence you want to embody

This layer anchors you. It helps keep you aligned, especially when things get busy or intense.

Relational Layer: What the group needs emotionally and energetically

- ❖ **Relational Purpose:** What this gathering might offer or acknowledge for everyone

- ❖ **Relational Intention:** The emotional tone that's asking to be cultivated

This keeps the celebration inclusive, feeling open, warm, resonant and engaging.

Event Layer: The wider symbolic meaning this celebration represents

- ❖ **Event Purpose:** The wider meaning or message the gathering represents

- ❖ **Event Intention:** The lasting feeling you want people to carry

This is where the event becomes more than an occasion; it becomes a story with lasting impact.

When you explore all three layers, your celebration becomes more than an event. It becomes a multidimensional experience that aligns individual insight, group energy and symbolic meaning.

The Purposeful Architect Stance

You adopt the stance of the Purposeful Architect, defining the soul of the experience. This invites you to slow down, listen inward and let the deeper meaning of the event emerge. You're not rushing into logistics; you're holding space, sketching the energetic foundation. Everything else flows from there.

Scenario: What This Looks Like in Practice

A Celebration Years in the Making

The brief sounds simple: "We'd love to organise something for our fifth anniversary." You pause before jumping into a hundred ideas. This isn't about logistics yet; it's about uncovering what truly matters.

When you meet the couple, they say, "We want a big party to bring everyone together and have a great time." But as you listen and sense in, their story unfolds. They eloped during lockdown. There was no celebration, no family gathered. One partner's parents still struggle with their same-sex marriage. A few friends quietly supported them, but there was never a moment of being fully seen.

A deeper truth emerges. "Yes, it is more than just a party," they say. "It's really about honouring our love, our resilience, the fact that we made it through, isn't it?"

Then, one adds quietly: "I think part of me still feels like we're not allowed to celebrate properly. Like our marriage was something to keep quiet about. We were never witnessed. Our families don't accept our relationship."

The atmosphere shifts. This is no longer just an anniversary party. It's a chance for visibility, healing and homecoming.

This is where clarity turns into design. Let's map the purpose and intention across all three layers.

The Three-Layer Purpose and Intention

❖ **Personal:** Create a meaningful experience that helps this couple feel fully seen, and hold the intention to stay present, curious and warm in how you guide them.

❖ **Relational:** Bring together supportive friends and hesitant family in genuine connection, with the intention of creating an atmosphere of ease and welcome.

❖ **Event:** Honour love through visibility – a declaration that this marriage deserves celebration, not silence – with the intention that everyone leaves feeling uplifted, connected and part of the story.

What Happened Here

You facilitated something sacred, not through technique, but through energy, presence and trust. You aligned and stayed open, holding space without trying to control it. And in that stillness, something true surfaced, something your clients had not even realised they were carrying until now. This is Celebration Alchemistry: transformation made possible through presence and intention.

Alchemiser's Arts in Action

Here's how the five Arts worked together in this moment:

- ❖ **Imagination** – Sensed what an inclusive celebration could feel like

- ❖ **Intuition** – Nudged you to hold space, sensing deeper story

- ❖ **Open Curiosity** – Kept you present through their pauses

- ❖ **Zenergy** – Felt vulnerability behind casual words

- ❖ **Visioning** – Glimpsed transformation possible through celebration

All five Arts work as an integrated system. You consciously draw on specific ones for different design aspects – but they're always present, supporting your work.

The Result

What started as a surface request became a deep foundation. The couple moved from "planning an anniversary party" to understanding this as a declaration of love and healing. They now have a Blueprint cornerstone – a clear purpose and intention that will guide every choice ahead.

SPARK Step P – Paint the Vision

Picture it before you plan it.

What This Step Does

This is about sensing into the celebration's full possibilities: the feeling, flow and emotional tone that bring your purpose and intention to life. You're sketching the experience before planning the logistics.

Vision is imagining something new and true – beyond trends, habits or spectacle. It's what keeps everyone inspired and aligned throughout the process, bringing colour and direction to everything that follows.

Painting The Vision

Vision isn't fixed, but felt, evolving as more details drop in when you hold space for it to unfold. You may feel unsteady at this stage. That's natural. This isn't conventional planning. It's softer, more expansive and far more intuitive. It's also deeply powerful.

Start where you are. Let your heart, not your head, lead, and let what truly matters come through. Sometimes what emerges is only a flicker, a colour or a feeling – hold that and more will come as you stay open to receive it.

Three Layers of Vision

To paint a rich and resonant vision, we explore what wants to emerge across the same three interconnected layers of Step S:

- ❖ **Personal Layer:** What you feel inspired to create as an authentic expression of your purpose and energetic signature.

    - → How might you show up at your best in this process?

    - → What would feel genuinely fulfilling for you to facilitate?

- ❖ **Relational Layer:** What might be possible when everyone's presence, energy and intentions combine.

    - → How might the alchemy of connection be animated through the experience?

    - → What could emerge when this particular group comes together?

- ❖ **Event Layer:** The defining concepts, moments and emotional story the celebration wants to tell.

    - → What's the energetic arc from beginning to end?

    - → What atmosphere and defining moments want to emerge?

These layers are synergistic; they interweave with purpose, building on each other and coming to life through mood, movement and magic.

The Intuitive Artist Stance

You adopt the stance of the Intuitive Artist, sensing the feel of the experience before its form. This invites you to trust what's emerging, hold it lightly and stay connected to its emotional essence. You're not planning; you're imagining. You're sensing the celebration's potential and allowing your creative instincts to guide what comes next, letting it emerge in its own time.

Scenario: What This Looks Like in Practice

Everyone takes a breath, settling after the depth of what has just been named: their purpose of being seen and honoured, their intention of creating ease and welcome. Gently, you explain that now it's time to get creative, to imagine how those truths might come to life in the celebration. "Not from the head, but from the heart," you remind them. This is not about logistics, but about letting images, feelings and possibilities rise.

At first, the room is quiet. You hold the pause and offer a few quiet prompts: "What atmosphere do you hope for? What kind of moments would feel most real?"

Slowly, ideas begin to surface. They describe wanting ease and fun, laughter alongside pockets of deeper conversation, a sense of belonging that includes both friends and family. They picture simple touches – candles, photo booth, live music – that could carry meaning without formality.

As they speak, you share a playful image of your own, something that captures joy and connection. It resonates instantly – something they had already been considering but had not voiced. That's the synergy and magic of shared vision. The picture is moving from abstract hopes to a felt possibility.

You then ask them to name the emotion they most want the celebration to embody. Their answers – "joy" and "freedom" – become the threads to weave through everything that follows.

You let them know you'll distil these threads into a living Celebration Blueprint, not a fixed plan but a touchstone they can return to. And you invite them to notice what else surfaces in the days ahead – a song, a colour, a memory – small clues that will continue to feed the vision.

The vision is now alive, held not as a checklist but as an energy. It has a pulse of its own.

What Happened Here

You guided collaborative sensing, allowing the celebration's soul to reveal itself organically. Rather than imposing a vision, you created conditions for their authentic vision to emerge. This is Celebration Alchemistry: vision through shared imagination.

Alchemiser's Arts in Action

Here's how the five Arts worked together in this moment:

- ❖ **Imagination** – Played with possibilities beyond the literal brief
- ❖ **Intuition** – Recognised when ideas resonated before they were fully voiced
- ❖ **Open Curiosity** – Stayed open to what wanted to emerge naturally
- ❖ **Zenergy** – Sensed the emotional tone beneath surface descriptions
- ❖ **Visioning** – Held the big picture while details began taking shape

Visioning and Intuition lead in this step, but all Arts collaborate to paint a vision that's both inspiring and true.

The Result

Their purpose began to find tangible form. The couple moved from understanding their deeper *why* to envisioning specific concepts, moments and atmosphere that would embody their emotional resonance of joy and freedom. They now have their creative palette, rich with colour and concrete elements that will bring their unique story to life.

SPARK Step A – Assess the Current Reality

Before you transform, you must be willing to see.

What This Step Does

Step A helps you pause regularly and assess what's actually happening versus what you hoped for. It keeps your Celebration Blueprint active as your compass.

This is about seeing clearly: what's progressing well, what's unclear, what needs attention. You're catching drift before it snowballs and appreciating what's already flowing – both matter for maintaining momentum.

This step isn't about taking a one-time pause; it's about building a practice. As an Alchemiser, you start to notice more in the moment. You'll also build in quick, personal scans, regular team check-ins and deeper client reflections as part of your process.

Creative vs Egoic Tension

Discomfort during assessment isn't bad – it might be *Creative Tension,* the stretch between where you are and what you're creating. This is what fuels inspired action.

But if discomfort pushes you into over-functioning (RAVE) or avoidance (FUNK), that's *Egoic Tension,* and it's not helpful. Use your A-Game or check-ins to recentre.

Three Layers of Assessment

To see clearly, we assess what's unfolding across the three interconnected layers. You'll recognise these from Steps S and P – the Personal, Relational and Event layers. This consistent framework helps you notice patterns and track how changes in one layer affect the others.

Personal Layer: Your inner state and energy as the process unfolds

> → Am I operating from Zilla Mode (rushed, controlling, perfectionist) or my Alchemiser Archetype (grounded, present, open)?

> → How is my current state affecting the process and the people involved?

Relational Layer: The collective dynamics and group energy

> → What's the emotional temperature? What's spoken and unspoken?

> → How are people engaging? What's creating connection or distance?

Event Layer: How the practical elements are tracking against your Blueprint

> → What's flowing naturally? What's feeling forced or misaligned?

> → Where does the energy match the intention, and where doesn't it?

The Truth Seeker Stance

You adopt the stance of the Truth Seeker, seeing clearly without flinching, with presence and purpose. Truth isn't always comfortable, but it's never the enemy. It's a release, a recalibration. You can't realign what you're not willing to see and spotlight.

This stance integrates your A-Game leadership approach

> **Arrive:** Pause and notice what's true for you first. When the soul stretches, the subconscious often scrambles for safety. That's when EGO (Excessive Grasping and Overthinking) kicks in. You might overcompensate or second-guess. Don't mistake that for failure, or a reason to stop. Resistance often means something meaningful is stirring; use it as Creative Tension to fuel you and your work.

Assess: Once you've anchored yourself, extend awareness outward. With people, you're tuning into the unspoken: the awkward silence, the shifting tone, the quiet glance. You're not here to control or manage; you're here to witness with steady presence and keep the energy honest.

With the practical flow of logistics, you're scanning for drift: a timeline that feels too tight, a decision made too quickly, a detail carrying more weight than it should. Not to micromanage, but to notice what needs attention before it unravels.

Using this stance helps create space for yourself, others and the process. You're not fixing, you're noticing. And that's where clarity begins. This clarity matters beyond your own role. Events that are meant to connect often leave people drained or disconnected, not because anyone lacks care, but because we skip over discomfort, avoid tension or miss the unspoken expectations beneath the surface. That's the real celebration crisis – the unspoken misunderstandings that divide us.

The Truth Seeker stance interrupts that pattern. As an organiser, you witness what others might overlook, notice where energy is drifting and name what's real. That's how you move from assumption to awareness, and how you begin to alchemise celebration for yourself and for everyone involved.

Scenario: What This Looks Like in Practice

It's been weeks since your session with the anniversary couple. You've crafted their Celebration Blueprint and sent it over, but heard nothing since. A niggle stirs. You pause and scan: *What's pulling my attention? What am I assuming?*

Up comes the old belief story: *Maybe I didn't do enough. Maybe it's (I'm) not good enough.* You name it for what it is: EGO's tap-tap to keep you in check, and then let it go. Centred and clear now.

They arrive appearing warm, but you sense some coolness beneath the surface. Without that check-in, you might've taken it personally. You ease into updates, then pause: "How are things on your end?"

A glance, then silence. You lean in slightly. *When something matters this much, it can stir up resistance – doubt, fear, overwhelm. It doesn't mean anything's wrong. It means something meaningful is happening.*

You slide their Celebration Blueprint across the table. "Remember this? The joy, the freedom. Let's revisit what you envisioned. What might be pulling you away from that?"

The space opens. One admits to overwhelm. The other, more quietly: "It's my parents … they're polite, but so cold and formal. I hoped they'd be different with this celebration. They're not."

You don't interrupt. You don't fix. You witness. You're creating space for what's underneath so the couple and their celebration can move forward with clarity and heart.

What Happened Here

You steadied yourself first, then witnessed what was real without rushing to fix. Your presence allowed the uncomfortable truth to surface and transform into useful clarity. This is Celebration Alchemistry: seeing through compassionate honesty.

Alchemiser's Arts in Action

Here's how the five Arts worked together in this moment:

- ❖ **Imagination** – Held space for new possibility beyond the discomfort
- ❖ **Intuition** – Sensed the coolness beneath the warm surface
- ❖ **Open Curiosity** – Asked without assumption, listening without rushing
- ❖ **Zenergy** – Read the room's emotional undercurrent accurately
- ❖ **Visioning** – Held the Blueprint steady while assessing drift

Zenergy, Intuition and Open Curiosity lead in this step, helping you see clearly without judgement or rushing to fix.

The Result

What began as uncomfortable tension became useful clarity. The couple reconnected with their deeper truth while acknowledging the challenges in play. You now have something solid to work with, not assumptions or wishful thinking: what's actually present.

Truth Seeker's Reality Check

A creative clarity scan for seeing what's true

Before moving forward with aligned action, you need clarity about what's really going on, energetically, emotionally, practically. The following practice helps surface what's supporting or distorting. Use it anytime you feel stuck, reactive or just want to reconnect with what matters.

Check in across four lenses:

→ **The Gold:** What's working well: for you, the team and the overall Blueprint? What's aligned, resourced or naturally flowing? Build from strength, not from scarcity.

→ **The Lead:** What's creating friction or distortion: doubts, logistics, egoic patterns? Lead isn't failure, it's potential waiting to be transformed.

→ **Creative Tension:** What's the stretch between where you are and where you want to be? Don't rush to resolve; sit with the tension. Ask: *What am I resisting or avoiding? What can I hold with curiosity instead of trying to fix?*

→ **EGO Check:** Are you in RAVE (overcomplicating, over-functioning) or FUNK (hesitating, deflating)? Notice how Zilla shows up here, the old patterns that pull you off course. What story or belief might be clouding your view?

Let clarity meet compassion. See what's true, not to fix it, but to understand. #MixNotFix

SPARK Step R – Realign Actions

Turning insight into aligned action.

What This Step Does

Step R takes your reality check findings and turns them into aligned action. You already track logistics and catch risks – this goes deeper, sensing energetic drift and unspoken tensions before they pull things off course.

Realignment means reconnecting to your Celebration Blueprint before acting. Sometimes it's a small nudge, sometimes a bold move. Whatever the scale, you're grounded in clarity, not driven by pressure or default reactions.

This step also creates space for honest dialogue. It's the pause before the pivot. Sometimes that pause leads to a quick adjustment in the middle of a conversation. Other times, it invites others into the solution, as part of a review meeting or process check.

The Goldsmith Stance

You adopt the stance of the "Goldsmith," refining what's already there rather than discarding what feels messy. You pause with purpose, returning to the Celebration Blueprint with focus and discernment, seeing what most needs attention now, letting the rest fall away.

You know the stretch between vision and reality carries value. This stance supports you in holding that Creative Tension steady, so it guides the next move, and the one after. It invites you to work with your Arts to drop beneath logic into deeper knowing.

This stance is grounded in your A-Game leadership approach

> **Align:** Pause to reconnect with energy, intention and purpose. Before you adjust anything outwardly, you realign inwardly, grounding yourself so you stay responsive and let choices flow from clarity, not pressure.

> **Activate:** From that alignment, you move into action, staying attuned to what's shifting and choosing how to evolve. You let the next steps arise naturally rather than through force.

The Goldsmith stance keeps your perspective steady and your presence strong, so every adjustment is made with integrity and care.

Scenario: What This Looks Like in Practice

You anchor them in the gold, reminding them of the joy and freedom they wanted this celebration to embody. You see one partner's head drop as she reconnects with their original vision.

Then she speaks slowly: "Coming in today ... I didn't want to do the ceremony in front of my parents. I wasn't even sure I wanted them there at all." Her voice cracks. "But now I realise this is about us, not them."

You hold the space, sensing this isn't a planning problem; it's transformation in motion. Instead of offering solutions, you invite them into stillness.

"Let's take a breath together. Feel into that joy and freedom, the essence of what this celebration means to you. Now bring the vision to mind: the music, the candlelight, the laughter. From that place of love and clarity, just see what's in front of you. Don't solve it yet; just breathe with it."

They come back to you transformed. Her eyes shine. The energy has shifted; the heaviness has lifted. You work together refining decisions with ease. Their Blueprint is alive again, aligned, clear and full of love.

What Happened Here

You held Creative Tension steady, letting it do the alchemical work. Instead of solving their problem, you trusted their own clarity to emerge. This is Celebration Alchemistry: change through holding frequency rather than pushing outcomes.

Alchemiser's Arts in Action

Here's how the five Arts worked together in this moment:

- ❖ **Imagination** – Held space for solutions beyond either/or thinking

- ❖ **Intuition** – Trusted the pause, knowing answers would arise

- ❖ **Open Curiosity** – Stayed with Creative Tension instead of collapsing it

- ❖ **Zenergy** – Invited them to breathe and feel into their truth

- ❖ **Visioning** – Reconnected them to joy and freedom at the heart of their Blueprint

All Arts converge in realignment, creating conditions for clarity to emerge rather than forcing solutions.

The Result

Tension transformed into clarity. The couple moved from either/or thinking to integrated understanding. They reconnected with their deeper truth while finding a way forward that honoured both their vision and current challenges. The Blueprint remained central, guiding authentic choices rather than impossible ideals.

⟋ Goldsmith's Realignment

A three-step process for moving from insight to aligned action

Use this process to transform Creative Tension into clarity. The three steps work together to ground you in what matters while opening space for aligned action.

Clear the Clutter: Release internal noise, assumptions, and anything clouding your Blueprint: thoughts, emotions, "shoulds," physical distractions, or inessential tasks.

Bridge Vision to Action: Reconnect with your Blueprint's emotional core, then feel the Creative Tension between dream and current reality. Don't rush to resolve; let the stretch guide you.

Refine and Define: From that reconnection, let aligned next steps emerge organically through presence rather than pressure. Trust what wants to arise from the Creative Tension you've been holding.

This isn't about forcing solutions or collapsing tension. It's about holding space so clarity can land, and authentic action can emerge. That's alchemy. That's what makes you a true Celebration Alchemiser.

SPARK Step K – Keep Legacy

The magic isn't just in the moment. It's in the journey from start to finish and beyond.

What This Step Does

Step K focuses on two interconnected elements: *legacy* (lasting impact) and *momentum* (the energy that keeps everything moving forward).

Legacy matters because meaning isn't automatic – it's designed. Momentum matters because without it, progress stalls, decisions drag and the experience feels heavy instead of alive with possibility.

When you make both a priority, you create *SPARK Synergy* – that multiplier effect we saw earlier – where all elements align, making the whole greater than the sum of its parts. This sets you apart professionally and builds resilience and reputation, while ensuring celebrations create lasting meaning rather than just successful logistics.

Sustaining Energy

Your energy matters more than ever at this stage. You've held a powerful vision and built a solid plan, but if you're running on empty, everything risks slipping into survival mode. This is where Zilla Mode can sneak in: RAVE (gripping too tightly, overdoing) or FUNK (pulling back, doubting, avoiding). This is where your practices – check-ins, pauses, A-game resets – become the fuel that keeps you steady and the celebration on course.

Steps A and R become your go-to tools for sustaining both legacy and momentum: regular check-ins prevent firefighting and keep energy steady rather than defaulting to "push through and tick boxes" mode.

When you lead from your Alchemising Archetype and manage your energy with intention, something shifts. You bring the celebration and its legacy home with strength and presence, so it doesn't just land – it lasts.

Four Layers of Legacy

Legacy ripples outward differently than purpose, intention or vision. While those earlier steps work across three interconnected layers, legacy expands into four concentric circles of impact – from your personal growth to cultural influence:

- ❖ **Personal Layer** – *Growth and Imprint:* How this process grows your skills, confidence and reputation. What you want it to say about how you work and connect. This is about *your* transformation through the work.

- ❖ **Relational Layer** – *Connection and Change:* How this experience affects group dynamics. Could it heal rifts, strengthen bonds or create new rituals that impact future connections? This is about how *relationships* shift.

- ❖ **Event Layer** – *Memory and Meaning:* The story this celebration tells and the message it leaves in hearts. Legacy felt, not forced. This is about the *event's* immediate emotional and symbolic impact.

- ❖ **Cultural Layer** – *Influence and Inspiration:* What this event might set in motion: new possibilities it could inspire, perspectives it might shift, quiet changes that ripple outward. This is about the *cultural* or *community* influence.

Legacy doesn't have to be grand. Sometimes the smallest act, done with intention, creates the biggest ripple across any or all four layers.

The Legacy Holder Stance

As a Celebration Alchemiser, the Legacy Holder stance is inherent to your role. This is how you protect the frequency of celebration from start to finish, ensuring design and energy work together to build meaningful impact – creating SPARK Synergy.

What this means in practice:

> → **At the start:** You sketch the first outline of legacy when you dig below the surface for the deeper purposes and possibilities.

> → **During design:** You stay open to ideas and opportunities that add depth and meaning, building legacy into both the process and the experience.

> → **In delivery:** You protect the Blueprint's energy, so what you've designed lands with integrity and impact.

This stance fuels momentum and gives you the ability to inspire, motivate and energise – not just yourself but everyone involved. It keeps you connected to the bigger picture, tapping into strength when challenges arise, tensions build and clear heads and hearts are called for.

Scenario: What This Looks Like in Practice

It starts with a message: *"Something's happened. Can we talk?"*

You jump on a video call. Their faces answer before words are spoken – they're radiant, close together on screen.

"My parents reached out," one says quietly. "Out of the blue. They'd been talking to their new minister. One thing he said changed everything: *'Judgement isn't love.'* They said they'd love to come, if we'll have them. They want to get to know us as a couple, to be part of our lives."

You sit with it. You know what this is: what happens when energy is held, when vision is protected, when you work with Creative Tension instead of collapsing it. This is SPARK Synergy in action.

The Four Layers Unfold:

→ **Personal:** Both partners navigated fear and old wounds, coming out more connected. You grew in how you held space and worked with Creative Tension.

→ **Relational:** Family dynamics shifted. A door opened that had been closed for years, changing future relationship possibilities.

→ **Celebration:** Their anniversary became a full expression of love and courage, a declaration of who they are, unfiltered and unapologetic.

→ **Cultural:** Their story rippled out. Someone at the celebration might witness a moment that shifts their own perspective on love, inclusion or courage.

What Happened Here

You protected the Blueprint's energy from start to finish, creating a container where transformation could unfold. This is Celebration Alchemistry: sustained presence that generates lasting impact.

Alchemiser's Arts in Action

Here's how the five Arts worked together throughout the journey:

❖ **Imagination** – Held possibility steady even when challenges arose

❖ **Intuition** – Trusted the Blueprint's thread through uncertainty

❖ **Open Curiosity** – Stayed open to unexpected transformation (parents' shift)

❖ **Zenergy** – Protected the celebration's frequency from start to finish

❖ **Visioning** – Helped the ripples extend beyond the immediate event

Visioning and Zenergy anchor this step, sustaining momentum and protecting meaning through delivery and beyond.

The Result

Legacy became a lived reality. What started as planning an anniversary party evolved into catalysing family healing and personal growth. The celebration's impact extended far beyond one evening, creating ripple effects that will influence relationships and perspectives for years to come. The Blueprint didn't just guide the event; it generated lasting transformation.

⁄ Completion Process – Closing One Chapter to Open the Next

One of the most powerful ways to close a celebration journey and anchor its legacy is through an intentional close or wrap-up. This isn't EGO's version of "thank goodness that's done." It's your Alchemising practice of honouring the full journey. Endings are transitions.

The Four Reflection Steps:

> → **What has been created?** Acknowledge what came into being, seen and unseen: the memories, atmosphere, impact.

> → **What has been learned?** What stretched you? What insights will be carried forward?

> → **What needs to be released?** What can be let go: old stories, expectations, lingering pressure? Energetic housekeeping for what's next.

> → **What's ready to emerge?** What seeds were planted? What's whispering for attention? Keep this soft; it's an invitation, not a to-do list.

Use this for any or all of the legacy levels. It can be a private journal moment, a shared debrief or a closing ritual. However it looks, the key is not to rush or force. Bring your Alchemiser's Arts into play, so you come from presence and heart – beyond logic or habit.

SPARK: A Living Cycle for Celebration Magic

You've walked through the five steps of SPARK: a process and practice that blends strategy with soul. Each step expands the others, creating flow that keeps energy vibrant, purpose anchored and legacy alive. Think of it as your creative compass, guiding you from concept through delivery and beyond. Return to it whenever clarity fades or momentum dips.

SPARK is more than a framework. The more you use it, the more powerful it becomes. Start small and experiment. Sketch your Blueprint. Try one step, one Stance or one Art. Notice what shifts when you pause for purpose instead of defaulting to the push for progress. That's where real change happens, one intentional move at a time.

The Alchemiser's Invitation

You may have started this section thinking, *I already know how to organise and design.* And you do. This isn't about replacing what you know; it's about adding a new dimension to your practice. Something different, maybe intangible at times, but deeply powerful.

Now you hold celebration as a frequency, a living vibration of joy, meaning and intention. You're bringing events to life as felt experiences, powered by presence, energy and soul. From thought leaders like Tahira Endean and Priya Parker, to grassroots organisers rewriting the rules, the call is clear: the future of celebration is intentional, human and deeply felt. This is your invitation to answer that call.

You already lead; people turn to you for this very reason. But too often, organisers neglect themselves, pouring out energy without replenishing it. That's where **Life Mixology** and **Celebration Alchemistry** come in. They put you at the centre, helping you sustain your leadership without losing your spark. When you work this way, you tap into a creative source that inspires, fulfils and transforms both you and your work.

Will it feel different? Yes. At times uncomfortable, because you're leaving familiar ground. But if you want work that is deeply yours and truly impactful, this is your path. The one shift that makes the biggest difference is adopting the stance of **Legacy Holder** – keeper of why what you're doing matters.

When you hold this stance, you grow your practice without burning out. Your presence becomes part of your reputation, not just for how well you deliver, but for how powerfully you hold space.

This is your invitation to step into your Alchemiser's Studio – whether imaginative or real – to claim that creative space where purpose, vision and energy meet. It's here your craft becomes something more, something magical. And you're only at the beginning of what's possible.

SECTION 5
Fizz, Flow and Full-Hearted Living

La Vie en Célébration: **When Joy Becomes Who You Are**

The famous song *"La Vie en Rose"* by Édith Piaf is about seeing the world through the lens of love, when everything feels luminous, effortless and beautiful because you're with someone you adore. My invitation to you now is this: *What if that special someone is you?*

What if the deep well of joy and fulfilment you've been seeking externally – in milestones, in others, in achievements – begins with self-appreciation and self-celebration? What if you became the one who sees life through the lens of beauty, love and wonder, because you've returned to your own radiant self?

When that becomes your foundation, everything else expands. Life begins to shimmer. You reconnect with the sacred in the ordinary. You move through your days with more ease, delight and joy.

Life becomes *la vie en célébration* – more than an occasion, a way to live.

Chapter 11
The Celebration (r)Evolution

A Return to Love, A Call to Wonder

You may not have known exactly why you picked up this book. Maybe it was timing. Maybe something deeper – a quiet whisper, a flicker of knowing, that celebration (and life?) had lost its fizz.

Some part of you remembered what it could be.

So, you brought it home (thank you!). Something in you stayed curious – a quiet longing to reconnect, not just to celebration, but to the spirit beneath it and to your own essence.

We've forgotten that celebration is something you feel, a frequency you connect with. It was never meant to be reserved for the big milestones alone; it's the everyday rhythm that opens us back up to life. True celebration is a living force of connection and joy, reminding us that we belong to ourselves and to each other.

This book invites a gentle (r)Evolution – a soulful return to yourself, to joy and to Celly, our Spirit of Celebration. Whether you organise events professionally, create gatherings at home or simply want to infuse more meaning into your days, the path is the same: shifting from something stressful you endure to something you live fully.

And while we've explored all this through the lens of celebration, everything we've covered holds true for life in general. How you behave when it matters, how you stay grounded when the stakes feel high, how you bring intention, alignment and maybe even a little magic to your creating. Because, as the saying goes: how you do one thing is how you do everything.

The Transformation

This transformation rests on the shifts we've explored: **Life Mixology** (how you show up for yourself and others) and **Celebration 2.0** (how you see and engage with celebration). When these meet – presence and practice – something bigger unfolds. **Celebration Alchemy:** where intention and awareness mix into something transformative.

Celebration Transformation at a Glance

Life Mixology 2.0 (inner alignment)

+

Celebration 2.0 (new approach)

=

Celebration Alchemy (magic happens!)

This alchemy creates four distinct shifts in how you experience life, what I call the "Four Promises" of living this way.

The Four Promises of Celebration Alchemy

These aren't goals to chase, but invitations that meet you where you are and deepen as you keep walking this path. Each comes with simple practices you can try today:

> ❖ **Power: Reclaim Your Energy, Redefine Your Impact**
>
> This isn't about control, it's about owning your presence: the energy you bring, because that energy colours everything. When you take responsibility for your state, that's real power, the shift from autopilot to living and leading purposefully.
>
> **Try This:** Before your next important interaction, pause and ask: *What energy do I want to bring here?* Notice how this simple question changes how you show up.

❖ **Pleasure: Savour What's Here, Now**

We've been taught to delay joy; save it for milestones, for "someday." But celebration is meant to be tasted daily. Pleasure softens life's edges and lets meaning sink in.

Try This: Set three "pleasure alerts" throughout your day: moments to pause and notice something you're enjoying right now, a warm cup of coffee, sunlight through the window, a text from someone you love.

❖ **Possibilities: Expand What's Possible Through Connection**

When you live with intention, new doors open. This is where Co-Celebration comes alive, when your energy sparks others and theirs sparks you. Trust grows, bonds deepen, legacy begins.

Try This: In your next conversation, bring full presence. Notice how being genuinely interested in someone else creates unexpected connections and opportunities.

❖ **Purpose: Create Meaning That Lasts**

Purpose isn't a grand mission you hunt for; it's meaning you weave into your days. When you approach life this way, you create experiences that matter now and build something worth celebrating.

Try This: End each day by asking yourself: *What mattered most today?* Let that guide tomorrow's choices.

Your Licence to Spill

If you'd like a playful way to anchor this mindset, you may recall my James Bond-inspired Licence to Spill: intentionally spill gratitude, wonder, delight and love into the corners that need it most. This puts us in a playful, curious and experimental frame of mind – it's how we step into being **SpillJoys.**

You know who you are – the ones who light up rooms, who see possibilities, who believe in joy's power. We're the ones who can't help but overflow with appreciation, who spark something in others just by being authentically ourselves.

As we explored in the "spillover effect," there's also the default, unconscious side when we spill our pain and struggle onto others. But what matters most is awareness. With it, we gain the freedom to notice, reset and choose joy again.

This is your permission slip to live this practice wherever you are, in whatever way feels true. Because the world needs more SpillJoys – Joy Catalysts who understand that spreading celebration, appreciation and joy isn't extra; it's essential.

My Cocktail of Joy

Since we've been talking about cocktails throughout this book, it feels right to include an actual one before we finish – and of course, a story with heart and a nice twist of serendipity.

It involves a solo road trip I'd dreamed of for years: San Francisco to LA, down the Pacific Coast Highway. This was me choosing presence over efficiency, beauty over the quickest route. No real plan, not even hotels booked. That choice felt like reclaimed power, reminding me that presence is always a choice.

As miles rolled by, pleasure found me everywhere: in slow curves, incredible bridges, ocean breezes, time with no agenda. Possibility showed up through unplanned detours, surprise discoveries, the simple joy of saying yes. Purpose hummed quietly, reminding me life isn't just about where you're going, but how you travel.

One stop stole my heart: San Luis Obispo, embodying the *SlowCal* way and their perfect slogan: "Life's Too Beautiful to Rush." The whole stay was magical, but one night particularly sparkled. Chatting with bartenders led to swapping stories and co-creating cocktails. Pure mixology fun! They surprised me by putting one of mine, Shiv's Elixir, on their menu.

Years later, wanting to share that moment here, I couldn't find the recipes. So, I reached out to my friend Astrid, the powerhouse behind Shed 5 in Wellington, New Zealand. She didn't just help recreate it; she made it sing.

And so, with gratitude to both crews, here it is, freshly shaken. A toast from my heart to yours.

Siobhán's Joy Elixir

My Joy Elixir

30 ml Malfy blood orange gin
15 ml Amaro Montenegro
10 ml cinnamon syrup
15 ml grapefruit juice
5 ml Campari
6 dashes rhubarb bitters

Garnish: Flamed orange

Add all ingredients to a shaker filled
with ice, infuse with intention

Shake briskly until chilled, letting
energy & possibility mingle

Strain into a chilled coupe

Express orange oils over the drink,
flame the peel & drop it in – a tiny kiss
to awaken the senses

Sip slowly. Toasting with joy &
presence
Share with the people you love &
appreciate

A celebration in a glass: citrusy, spiced, bittersweet and bold.

The Heart of It All

That sip captures the essence of everything this book stands for: appreciation, joy and connection. Because what matters most is love – giving it, receiving it and letting it infuse us with awe and wonder.

Love is what makes us feel most alive, not the grand gestures, but the small, real moments of appreciation. A look that says, *I see you.* A conversation that lingers. A presence that says, *I'm here.*

Wonder keeps magic alive. It's awe and curiosity. It's the spark that reminds us to look again, to notice, to feel the extraordinary in the ordinary.

When we live from this place, we step into our true potential: Celebration Alchemists – turning life's lead into the gold of joy.

That's the heart of Celebration Alchemy: a more joyful way to live, gather and create moments that matter. Because life's too short not to!

Where do you go from here?

Not to perfection. Not to "version 2.0" overnight. Life Mixology isn't about quick fixes; it's about curiosity, experimentation and compassion. We've uncovered lots of practices and tools. The main thing is to keep it easy and start small. Use the simple act of appreciation to support you:

> *That felt good. How lucky am I? Wow, look at that.*

Over time, these moments chip away at old patterns and create space for something softer, lighter, more aligned. You might notice quiet shifts seeping in: celebrating small wins, being gentler in messy moments, feeling less rushed, more present.

Keep choosing the next small step. Try one thing and notice what changes. Because that's what a Celebration Alchemist does – works with what's already there, not to fix but to refine.

You're already enough. You're already worthy. Now you get to remember – and let that remembering spill into everything you touch.

The Journey

You've walked a path of reconnection: to joy, presence and soulful living. Along the way, you've seen how habitual ways of living and celebrating hold us back and how much more is possible when we choose to appreciate, create and celebrate with intention.

This isn't an ending; it's an opening. Take what calls to you now; the rest will be here when you're ready. There's no rush, no expiry date.

This journey I've shared has been my own, learning to come home to myself through appreciation, celebration and joy. My passion has always been to make a difference, to be the change, to serve something greater than me.

I've discovered we are more than we've been conditioned to believe. We have more love, more joy, more potential than we ever allowed ourselves to imagine. All we need to do is choose to see it – and use it. And in sharing it, we multiply it.

That's the heart and soul of this book. It's my wish, my hope and my ask:

Spill Joy. Spread Love. Share Magic.

One moment of celebration, like a single breath across dandelion seeds, sends love rippling further than you'll ever know

When you embody celebration and practice appreciation, you show up with presence and generosity – you cultivate Joytality. Like seeds or wishes carried on the breeze, this energy sends ripples of love further than you'll ever know. It's the quiet power behind true celebration – exactly what the world needs most right now.

The Spirit of Celebration is part of this frequency, here to lift, guide, and remind us of the wonder that's always been ours.

Here's a little note from her heart to yours as you step into what comes next.

A Love Note from Celly

Dear One,

You've made it here – through reflection, through feeling, through staying open. That's all I'll ever ask of you.

I'm not something you need to find. I've always been here, just beneath the noise, the pressure, the doing.

I live in your laughter, your pauses, your tears, your joy. In your giggles, like a child splashing in puddles. In the goosebumps of a perfect sunset. In the lump in your throat as someone you love moves on.

I've whispered to you through music, through movement. Through that tiny skip in your heart when you felt fully, radiantly alive.

Every time you choose appreciation, connection and joy, you'll feel me more deeply. Celebrate the you who is already enough. Celebrate the small things, make them matter.

Let yourself be moved. Let yourself be seen.

That's what celebration really is: a return to you, to what matters. To what's always been true.

I'll be here in the shimmer, in the moment that makes your heart swell, and in the next, the one after that.

With love,

Celly

EPILOGUE
A Final Toast to My Dad

There have been other "spirits" with me on this journey: my loved ones who are no longer here, whose love of life continues to inspire me.

One of them, my dad Derry, deserves a final toast. He was the soul of celebration in our family: a man who believed in music, stories and the magic of connection. Nothing gave him more joy than a gathering, a sing-song and a shared glass of Powers Irish whiskey. Our simple toast was always: *"More power(s) to you."* He also loved the Irish language, and his favourite toast follows. But before that, I want to share a piece of the tribute I wrote for Mom, after he'd died, because it captures who he was and why he mattered so much to us.

Dad, Derry – "Popsicle" (as I called him later in life)

> In the light, you always shone bright.
> Whistling at your work.
> Gifted hands, always busy – making, mending, creating, providing.
> A craftsman. A problem-solving engineer.
>
> Deeply connected to nature,
> The lowing of a cow, the call of a bird,
>
> All worthy of your quiet reverence.
>
> Warm, melodic singing,
>
> Cheeky grin, mischievous eyes,
> Happiest in the midst of a sing-along,

Rousing voices, stories flowing,

Life and soul of every gathering.

Boundless generosity,
Kindling our fires and our hearts,
Metaphorically, physically.

Blessed with intelligence,
Your mind a revelation

Reciting poems, stories, passages
With perfect pitch and dramatic flair,
Effortlessly. Impressively.

A global citizen long before the phrase was coined.
A son, a brother, an uncle, a father,
A proud granddad in exaltation.

Strong. Mighty. Gentle.
An amazing brain, a big heart.

So, Dad, I toast you now, as we always did. With a wee drop of the "God" stuff – *"more power(s) to you!"* And you'd respond:

> *"Go mbeirimid beo ar an am seo arís,*
> *agus go mbeirimid go léir le chéile."*
>
> *("May we live this time again, and may we all be together.")*

And so, until we all meet again, Pops

> *Ar dheis Dé go raibh d'anam dílis*
> *(May your faithful soul be at God's right hand.)*

Thank you, Dad. Thank you, family.

And thank you, dear Reader, for walking this journey with me. And for helping to keep the Spirit of Celebration present in your own way.

Thank You!

I'm so grateful you chose to join me on this journey.

If the spirit and magic of *Celebration Alchemy* have stirred something in you, scan the QR code below for resources, updates and ways to connect.

Scan the QR Code Here:

Want to go deeper? I'd love to stay connected:

www.celebrationalchemy.com

hello@celebrationalchemy.com

There are exciting things in the works – training, retreats, and yes … #HaveBookWillTravel. If you'd like to bring this work to your organisation, community, or event, let's talk.

Your feedback means the world to me. I'd love it if you shared your thoughts in a review on Amazon. Your words help others discover this work and spread the message of meaning, magic and more joy.

Thank you for being part of this Celebration Movement.

Celebration Alchemy A-Z Glossary

A

A-Game (Your): Organising leadership in action. A guide to showing up intentionally when it matters, grounded, calm and responsive. Choosing presence over panic and clarity over chaos. Consists of five steps: Arrive, Assess, Align, Activate, and Anchor. *See: Celebration Alchemiser.*

Alchemiser Archetype (Your): Your SOUL-aligned organising style, inspired by Enneagram types. Reflects your strengths and provides a growth path for how you design, lead and energise celebration. Each Archetype has a paired EGO-driven Zilla Mode, showing the contrast between reactive, default habits and intentional, empowered leadership. *See: Organising Style, SOUL FLOW; Zilla Mode.*

Alchemiser's A-Game Oracle (Your): *See: Oracle.*

Alchemiser's Studio (The): An Alchemiser's creative sanctuary, literal or metaphorical, for intentional celebration design. The space where purpose, vision and energy meet, and where the SPARK framework, Arts, Stances and Alchemising Cocktail come alive. The threshold from reactive planning to creative alchemy.

Alchemising: The act of transformational event design through aligned energy, awareness and intention, using innate capabilities and resources. *See: Celebration Alchemistry, Celebration Alchemiser.*

Alchemising Cocktail (Your): Complete energetic signature as an organiser. The full blend in motion. The internal mix and external presence brought to celebration design and leadership. *See: Signature Mix, Celebration Cocktail, Co-Celebration Style, and Organising Style.*

Alchemist's Way: *See: Way, The Celebration Alchemist.*

Arts, Alchemiser's: Energetic capabilities that support and guide soulful celebration design: **Imagination** – Wonder and play, **Intuition** – Inner knowing, **Open Curiosity** – Spacious inquiry, **Zenergy** – Emotional momentum, **Visioning** – Creative convergence. *See: Celebration Alchemiser.*

B

Blueprint, Celebration: *See Celebration Blueprint*

Bottle (The): A metaphor for you – the vessel holding your unique life mix (your blend of components, state and energy). What's inside is your *Signature Mix:* emotions, beliefs, habits, fears, hopes and stories. Its "temperature" reflects your operating state: EGO (explosive in RAVE or flat/frozen in FUNK) or SOUL (effervescent and flowing in FLOW). *See: Life Mixology, Signature Mix.*

C

Celebration Alchemy: The art and practice of bringing appreciation and joy into everyday life by adopting celebration as a mindset. It's also the transformation of shared moments through conscious presence, Co-Celebration and joyful contribution. In essence, it's turning the ordinary into extraordinary so that meaning, connection and joy become part of how we live and how we celebrate together. *The Celebration Alchemist's Way* is how you put this philosophy into practice.

Celebration Alchemist: Someone who embraces Celebration 2.0 as both a mindset and way of being. Present, intentional and appreciative, they choose their state, their energy and how they show up. A Joy Catalyst who creates meaning through alignment and connection, embodying the Spirit of Celebration in life, relationships and #MakingMomentsMatter. *See: Spirit of Celebration; Way, The Celebration Alchemist.*

Celebration Alchemistry: The intentional way of designing celebrations so they feel truly vibrant, connected and meaningful. It's the alchemical touch that takes an event from good to great, adding meaning, magic and joy to both the journey and the celebration itself.

Celebration Alchemiser: You, in your role as an organiser. You blend intention, energy and presence to design not just what happens, but how it feels and why it matters. You lead the process in a way that keeps people connected, the purpose clear, and the atmosphere alive, so every stage, from planning to the final moment, builds something people will remember and cherish. *See: Organising Style, Alchemising Cocktail.*

Celebration Blueprint: Your event's living North Star. Created through the first SPARK steps, it captures four essential elements: **Purpose** (the deeper why), **Intention** (the guiding energy), **Vision** (the possibility landscape) and **Legacy** (the lasting impact). The energetic foundation that keeps intention and action aligned throughout the celebration journey. *See: SPARK Synergy Framework, SPARK Synergy, Spirit of Celebration.*

Celebration Cocktail (Your): The energy brought when showing up to celebrate. How you "gear up" to meet others, consciously or on autopilot. Includes expectations, assumptions and any lingering residue from the day. What others begin to sense before you say a word. Your vibe and presence, flavoured by how you've prepared energetically (or not). *See: Signature Mix (your).*

Celebration Crisis (The): The modern-day disconnection from authentic celebration, characterised by pressure, performance and polarities. When celebration becomes more stressful than joyful, more about appearances than appreciation, and more draining than nourishing. The foundation of Celebration 1.0 and the reason for reimagining celebration through Celebration 2.0. *See: Celebration 1.0, Celebration 2.0.*

Celebration 1.0: Performance, pressure and polarities. A modern celebration crisis driven by external expectations, demands and emotional extremes, which leaves us disconnected from ourselves, from each other and from joy.

Celebration 2.0: Power, pleasure, possibilities and purpose. A new paradigm where celebration is both a mindset and a daily practice – intentional, soulful and life-affirming. Anchored in appreciation, presence and authentic connection, it's a way to heal, belong and live joyfully.

Celebration (r)Evolution (The): The conscious evolution from pressure and performance *(Celebration 1.0)* to presence and purpose *(Celebration 2.0)*. A reimagining of how we live, gather and connect, returning to appreciation and joy as a way of being. Celebration becomes an everyday essential, building momentum into a collective movement as more of us choose to live this way.

Celly: *See Spirit of Celebration.*

CHEERS: A touchstone to anchor appreciation: **C**hoose to **H**onour the moment, **E**mbrace it, **E**ngage it, **R**eflect on its meaning and **S**avour (and **S**hare it). *See: Everyday Infusions.*

Co-Celebration: The conscious choice to contribute your presence and energy to a shared celebration. It's the shift from being a passive attendee (1.0) to an active participant (2.0), a co-creator of atmosphere, meaning and joy. Whether you're lively or low-key, you help influence how the experience feels for everyone. This is the true expression of celebration as connection.

Co-Celebration Style (Your): How you actually interact, not just what you intend to bring, but what others experience. This is your relational impact. Do you energise or overwhelm? Withdraw or over-give? It's about the tone and energy you bring into the space, how you include and connect with others, or unintentionally disrupt the flow during shared celebration. *See: Celebration 2.0.*

Components, Human Experience: The inner elements shared by all, but primed differently in each person. These determine how your unique Life Mix works. They include: Personality, Mindset, Beliefs and Perceptions, Thinking Self, Emotions, Feelings, Mood, Behaviours and Habits. *See: Life Mixology.*

Consciousness: Four levels, each influencing awareness and experience: **Unconscious:** Deep conditioning and instinct; **Subconscious:** Emotional patterns and belief systems that run automatically, outside of awareness; **Conscious:** Present awareness and intentional choice; and **Superconscious:** Higher wisdom, insight and alignment. *See: Life Mixology.*

Creative Tension: The energising gap between where you are now (current reality) and where you want to be (vision). This tension is creative fuel – the stretch that motivates reflection, sparks insight and guides inspired action. When held with curiosity rather than collapsed through force, it becomes the generative space where your best ideas emerge. A key concept in the Alchemiser's Studio and SPARK process. *See: Alchemiser's Studio, SPARK Synergy Framework, Egoic Tension.*

D

Dimensions (3) of Celebration Alchemy: The ways you live and express Celebration 2.0 in real life:

> **Embrace:** Inner alignment and willingness to live from SOUL,

> **Express:** Infusing everyday moments with presence and appreciation, and

> **Engage:** Co-creating joyful and meaningful shared experiences

See: Way, The Celebration Alchemist.

E

EGO (Excessive, Grasping and Overthinking): Your fear-driven survival state. Shows up in variations between two extreme modes:

> **RAVE:** Reactive, Agitated, Validation-seeking, Escaping; and

> **FUNK:** Fearful, Unmotivated, Numb, Keeping small.

Egoic Tension: The uncomfortable, unhelpful tension that pushes you into over-functioning (RAVE mode) or avoidance (FUNK mode). Unlike Creative Tension, which fuels insight, Egoic Tension drains energy and pulls you away from alignment. The key is recognising the difference: Creative Tension feels like a stretch; Egoic Tension feels like stress. *See: Creative Tension, EGO, RAVE, FUNK.*

Elements, Core (5) of Celebration: The energetic foundation of Celebration Alchemy and central to Celebration 2.0 and Celly's presence. These five forces influence how celebration feels, flows and transforms:

Energy: The dynamic force that moves through and between us

Intention: The compass that guides meaning and focus

Alignment: The harmony between inner truth and outer expression

Presence: The choice to be here, now, fully engaged

Joy: The soul-fuel that makes celebration feel alive, nourishing and true

See: (Five) 5ALIVE for a practical tool to check and balance these energies.

Enneagram: A personality framework that reveals core motivations, habits and both stress and growth paths. In this book, it's used to understand how your Inner Mix appears in SOUL alignment or in EGO, and as the foundation for your Celebration Cocktail, Co-Celebration Style and Organising Style.

Everyday Infusions: Small, intentional acts that flavour daily life with appreciation and meaning. Little drops that turn ordinary moments into ones that feel alive and worth savouring. #MakingMomentsMatter. Part of *Express Dimension of Celebration Alchemy.*

F

(Five) 5ALIVE: A quick self-check tool based on the Five Core Elements of Celebration. Aligned, Live (Present), Intentional, Vital (Joy), and Energy. Used to check your presence and energy before, during, or after a celebration.

Five Shifts: Five reframes that transform how we see and experience celebration, moving from Celebration 1.0 to Celebration 2.0:

1. Celebration isn't a luxury; it's a necessity for life, connection and resilience.
2. Celebration isn't meaningful without intention.
3. Celebration isn't just about achievement; it's about alignment and integration.

4. You don't have to feel joyful to celebrate; celebration creates joy.
5. Celebration isn't genuine without appreciation as its foundation.

Together, these shifts help undo outdated beliefs and position celebration as essential, transformational and rooted in what truly matters. See: Celebration 2.0, Five Steps (The 5 S's).

Five Steps (The 5 S's), Alchemist's Way: The practical framework for living Celebration 2.0 in daily life:

1. **Start with You** (check your state)
2. **Select Your Ingredients** (choose how you want to show up)
3. **Stir with Intention** (move with purpose)
4. **Savour the Sip** (embrace the moment)
5. **Share the Sparkle** (be a Joy Catalyst)

These steps help you embody celebration as a way of being, not just something you do. *See: Way, The Celebration Alchemist; Celebration 2.0.*

#FizzByDesign: The proactive sparkle. Where #MixNotFix is about tuning inward, this is about showing up outwardly with purpose. Celebration on purpose, bringing energy, intention and fizz (your unique joy) into the moment and sparking it for others as a joy catalyst.

FLOW: Flexible, Light, Optimistic, Willing. The natural, expansive way you move through life when you're in your SOUL state, meeting life with ease, joy and openness to what's next. *See: SOUL.*

FUNK: Fearful, Unmotivated, Numb, Keeping small. A contracted, protective mode within the EGO state where energy shuts down, motivation fades and you retreat from possibility. *See: EGO.*

G

Glass (Your): Your capacity to hold and savour joy and celebration. Its "state" – whether full, cracked, overflowing or running low – affects how much you can take in and sustain. Linked to overall well-being, your glass reflects both your readiness and ability to experience life's moments fully. *See: Life Mixology.*

J

Joy Catalyst: Someone who doesn't just feel joy, but actively creates it. Through presence, energy and care, they lift a room, shift the mood and help others see possibility, even in challenging moments. They hold space for the light without denying the dark. #FizzByDesign. *See: Celebration Alchemist, SPLASH Effect, Licence to Spill, SpillJoy, Spillover Effect.*

Joytality: The vibrant mix of joy and vitality that comes from living and celebrating in soul alignment. It's the energy you can feel, and others can sense when you're fully alive, present and connected to what matters.

L

Legacy: The lasting impact of your choices, actions and presence, what remains after the event is over. In Celebration Alchemy, legacy is about meaning as much as memory, considered through different lenses or layers (e.g. personal, relational, event, cultural) for the most impactful result. A core focus of the SOUL state and the "Keep Legacy" step of SPARK. *See: SOUL, SPARK Synergy Framework.*

Licence to Spill: Playful permission to let joy and appreciation flow freely, without waiting for the perfect moment. Inspired by the spillover effect in psychology, it's the reminder that our energy always spills outward, so why not spill joy intentionally? *See: Celebration Alchemist, SPLASH Effect, Joy Catalyst, SpillJoy, Spillpain Mode, Spillover Effect.*

Life Mixology: A method for understanding yourself and how you operate, based on the #MixNotFix philosophy: you're not broken or in need of fixing; you already have the ingredients you need. The aim is to grow awareness of which state you're in, EGO or SOUL, and work with it consciously. Your **Signature Cocktail** is your inner mix in either state; your **Celebration Cocktail** is how that mix shifts as you prepare to meet and connect with others. Life Mixology is the foundation for Celebration Alchemy because when you understand how you operate and engage, you become conscious of, and more intentional about, your energy and impact.

Life Mixology 101: The operating manual for understanding your components, recognising your state and working with your mix to choose the behaviours and energy you bring.

Life Mixology 1.0: Default, EGO-driven mix: reactive, externally led and unbalanced. You operate from variations between EGO's two extreme modes, RAVE or FUNK, which influence how you think, feel and behave. *See: EGO.*

Life Mixology 2.0: Intentional, SOUL-led mix: purposeful, values-aligned and grounded in appreciation. You choose behaviours and energy that create joy and meaning as a natural part of daily life. *See: SOUL and FLOW.*

M

#MakingMomentsMatter: An everyday invitation to infuse life with meaning. Through presence, appreciation and small acts of noticing, you create moments that lift and linger. *See: Celebration 2.0.*

#MixNotFix: You're not broken, and you're not starting from scratch. You already have everything you need within you. The work is to remix it with greater awareness, appreciation and self-kindness. *See: Life Mixology.*

O

Oracle (Your Alchemising Oracle): Also called your Alchemiser's A-Game Oracle. A living companion for SOUL-aligned leadership. A real-time guide for navigating pressure, shifting your state and returning to presence. Includes your core leadership components, which you can use as a touchstone to design, lead and close celebrations with clarity and care. *See: Alchemiser's A-Game, Alchemiser's Arts, Alchemising Cocktail.*

Organising Style (Your): How you structure, lead and manage energy when organising a celebration. Based on Enneagram type and influenced by your operating state, either in Zilla Mode (EGO) or Alchemiser Archetype (SOUL FLOW). *See: Zilla Mode, Alchemiser Archetype, Celebration Alchemiser.*

R

RAVE: **R**eactive, **A**gitated, **V**alidation-seeking, **E**scaping. The overdrive mode within the EGO state. See: EGO.

S

SCARF: A neuroscience-based model by David Rock outlining five social triggers that influence human behaviour: **Status, Certainty, Autonomy, Relatedness and Fairness.** Our brains constantly scan for these cues, reading each as either a threat or a reward. SCARF helps explain why people may resist change, or even celebration, despite its positive intent. *See: Life Mixology.*

Shadow: The hidden ingredient in your mix: suppressed pain, untapped strengths and unconscious patterns that influence how you show up, often without you realising it, in either EGO or SOUL states. *See: Life Mixology.*

Signature Mix (Your): Your inner blend of thoughts, emotions, habits, beliefs and instincts, primed by your current state (EGO or SOUL). It's the flavour inside your "bottle" that influences how you think, feel and act before you engage with others. This is the first mix in Life Mixology. *See: Bottle, Life Mixology.*

SNAP: A quick reset tool to shift from EGO to SOUL: **S**ense in, **N**ame the story, **A**sk a better question, **P**ivot. *See: Life Mixology, Celebration 2.0.*

SOUL: (Self-Aware, Open-Hearted, Unique, Legacy-Focused): Your aligned Core Essence state. Expressed through FLOW: Flexible, Light, Optimistic and Willing. *See: Life Mixology, FLOW.*

SPARK Synergy Framework: The five-step intentional design process: **S:** Set Purpose and Intention, **P:** Paint the Vision, **A:** Assess Current Reality, **R:** Realign Actions, **K:** Keep Legacy and Momentum. *See: Celebration 2.0, Celebration Blueprint.*

SPARK Synergy: The multiplier effect that happens when the five SPARK steps work as a connected sequence, strengthening each other. When energy, purpose and thoughtful design flow together with Alchemising intention, the whole becomes greater than the sum of its parts. This is what brings the Celebration Blueprint to life, creating moments that resonate deeper, land truer and last longer. *See: SPARK Framework, Celebration Blueprint, Celebration Alchemistry.*

SpillJoy: Someone who overflows with appreciation and authentic presence, spreading joy into the spaces and people around them. A living expression of Celebration 2.0. The opposite of spillpain mode. *See: Joy Catalyst, Licence to Spill, Celebration 2.0; SPLASH Effect, Spillpain Mode, Spillover Effect.*

Spillover Effect (The): A psychological term describing how our inner state leaks into the spaces and relationships around us. In Celebration Alchemy, this explains both spillpain mode (when unprocessed hurt dampens joy) and SpillJoys (when appreciation and presence overflow and lift others). Awareness of the spillover effect is what gives us choice. *See: Licence to Spill, SpillJoy, Spillpain Mode, Joy Catalyst.*

Spillpain Mode: When hurt or strain spills outward, often unconsciously, and dampens joy. It doesn't mean someone is a pain; it means they're in pain. Too often judged or dismissed as "killjoys," but really a survival pattern spilling out. *See: Licence to Spill, Spillover Effect, SpillJoy, Celebration Alchemist.*

Spirit of Celebration (The/Your): Joyful, sacred and a little mischievous, **Celly** holds the energy of appreciation, vitality and connection. More than a symbol, she is an energetic guide back to your essence – a reminder that celebration is your natural state. She sparks joy, steadies your presence and helps you return to what matters most.

SPLASH Effect (The): The impact you create when showing up soul-aligned in Joy Catalyst mode. Your energy moves beyond you, touching others, colouring moments and leaving a lasting imprint of joy. SPLASH stands for: Spill joy, Pause for pleasure, Laugh out loud, Activate magic, Share generously, and Have fun. *See: Celebration Alchemist, Licence to Spill, Joy Catalyst, SpillJoy.*

Stances (5), Alchemiser: The five energetic perspectives that guide you through the SPARK steps:

> **Purposeful Architect** – holds the deeper why and energetic foundations,

> **Intuitive Artist** – translates energy into creative vision,

> **Truth Seeker** – brings honest awareness with compassion,

> **Goldsmith** – aligns action with purpose through detail,

> **Legacy Holder** – ensures meaning and momentum carry forward.

See: Celebration Alchemiser, Alchemiser's Arts, SPARK Synergy Framework, SPARK Synergy.

Studio (The): *See: Alchemiser's Studio (The)*

W

Way, The Celebration Alchemist: The practical application of Celebration Alchemy – how you live the philosophy through your choices, presence and energy. It works with the three Dimensions of Celebration Alchemy and comes to life through the Five Steps of the Alchemist's Way: Start with You, Select Your Ingredients, Stir with Intention, Savour the Sip and Share the Sparkle. It's about embodying *Joytality* and #MakingMomentsMatter as a daily practice, by choice, not obligation. *See: Celebration Alchemy, Celebration Alchemist, Dimensions.*

#WhatIf: A mindset of curiosity and courageous reimagining. It invites wonder, challenges complacency and opens the door to new possibilities.

Z

Zilla Mode: EGO-driven organiser state – can be perfectionist, avoidant, controlling or shut down. Highlights the reactive habits that pull you away from intentional, empowered leadership in celebration design, i.e., your Alchemiser Archetype. *See: Organising Style, Alchemiser Archetype.*

Zilla Zone: The impact of being in Zilla Mode. Others pick up on the tension, confusion or flatness you create, often without realising why. *See: Organising Style, Zilla Mode.*